BioCritiques

Bloom's BioCritiques

F. SCOTT FITZGERALD

Edited and with an introduction by
Harold Bloom
Sterling Professor of the Humanities
Yale University

CHELSEA HOUSE PUBLISHERS
Philadelphia

©2002 by Chelsea House Publishers, a subsidiary of
Haights Cross Communications.

Introduction © 2001 by Harold Bloom.

Printed and bound in the United States of America

10 9 8 7 6 5 4 3 2 1

Library of Congress Cataloging-in-Publication Data

F. Scott Fitzgerald / edited and with an introduction by Harold Bloom.
    p. cm. - (Bloom's bio critiques)
    Includes bibliographical references and index.
    ISBN 0-7910-6176-0
    1. Fitzgerald, F. Scott (Francis Scott), 1896-1940—Criticism and interpretation. I
Bloom, Harold. II. Series.

PS3511.I9 Z6137 2001
813'.52—dc21   2001053902

Chelsea House Publishers

1974 Sproul Road, Suite 400
Broomall, PA 19008-0914

http://www.chelseahouse.com

CONTENTS

USER'S GUIDE

These volumes are designed to introduce the reader to the life and work of the world's literary masters. Each volume begins with Harold Bloom's essay "The Work in the Writer" and a volume-specific introduction also written by Professor Bloom. Following these unique introductions is an engaging biography that discusses the major life events and important literary accomplishments of the author under consideration.

Furthermore, each volume includes an original critique that not only traces the themes, symbols, and ideas apparent in the author's works, but strives to put those works into a cultural and historical perspectives. In addition to the original critique is a brief selection of significant critical essays previously published on the author and his or her works followed by a concise and informative chronology of the writer's life. Finally, each volume concludes with a bibliography of the writer's works, a list of additional readings, and an index of important themes and ideas.

HAROLD BLOOM

The Work in the Writer

Literary biography found its masterpiece in James Boswell's *Life of Samuel Johnson*. Boswell, when he treated Johnson's writings, implicitly commented upon Johnson as found in his work, even as in the great critic's life. Modern instances of literary biography, such as Richard Ellmann's lives of W. B. Yeats, James Joyce, and Oscar Wilde, essentially follow in Boswell's pattern.

That the writer somehow is in the work, we need not doubt, though with William Shakespeare, writer-of-writers, we almost always need to rely upon pure surmise. The exquisite rancidities of the Problem Plays or Dark Comedies seem to express an extraordinary estrangement of Shakespeare from himself. When we read or attend *Troilus and Cressida* and *Measure for Measure*, we may be startled by particular speeches of Ulysses in the first play, or of Vincentio in the second. These speeches, of Ulysses upon hierarchy or upon time, or of Duke Vincentio upon death, are too strong either for their contexts or for the characters of their speakers. The same phenomenon occurs with Parolles, the military impostor of *All's Well That Ends Well*. Utterly disgraced, he nevertheless affirms: "Simply the thing I am/Shall make me live."

In Shakespeare, more even than in his peers, Dante and Cervantes, meaning always starts itself again through excess or overflow. The strongest of Shakespeare's creatures—Falstaff, Hamlet, Iago, Lear, Cleopatra—have an exuberance that is fiercer than their plays can contain. If Ben Jonson was at all correct in his complaint that "Shakespeare wanted art," it could have been only in a sense that he may not have intended. Where do the personalities of Falstaff or Hamlet touch a limit? What was it in Shakespeare that made the two parts of *Henry IV* and *Hamlet* into "plays unlimited"? Neither Falstaff nor Hamlet will be stopped: their wit, their beautiful, laughing speech, their intensity of being—all these are virtually infinite.

In what ways do Falstaff and Hamlet manifest the writer in the work? Evidently, we can never know, or know enough to answer with any authority. But what would happen if we reversed the question, and asked: How did the work form the writer, Shakespeare?

Of Shakespeare's inwardness, his biography tells us nothing. And yet, to an astonishing extent, Shakespeare created our inwardness. At the least, we can speculate that Shakespeare so lived his life as to conceal the depths of his nature, particularly as he rather prematurely aged. We do not have Shakespeare on Shakespeare, as any good reader of the Sonnets comes to realize: they do not constitute a key that unlocks his heart. No sequence of sonnets could be less confessional or more powerfully detached from the poet's self.

The German poet and universal genius, Goethe, affords a superb contrast to Shakespeare. Of Goethe's life, we know more than everything; I wonder sometimes if we know as much about Napoleon or Freud or any other human being who ever has lived, as we know about Goethe. Everywhere, we can find Goethe in his work, so much so that Goethe seems to crowd the writing out, just as Byron and Oscar Wilde seem to usurp their own literary accomplishments. Goethe, cunning beyond measure, nevertheless invested a rival exuberance in his greatest works that could match his personal charisma. The sublime outrageousness of the Second Part of *Faust*, or of the greater lyric and meditative poems, form a Counter-Sublime to Goethe's own daemonic intensity.

Goethe was fascinated by the daemonic in himself; we can doubt that Shakespeare had any such interests. Evidently, Shakespeare abandoned his acting career just before he composed *Measure for Measure* and *Othello*. I surmise that the egregious interventions by Vincentio and Iago displace the actor's energies into a new kind of mischief-making, a fresh opening to a subtler playwriting-within-the-play.

But what had opened Shakespeare to this new awareness? The answer is the work in the writer, *Hamlet* in Shakespeare. One can go further: it was not so much the play, *Hamlet*, as the character Hamlet, who changed Shakespeare's art forever.

Hamlet's personality is so large and varied that it rivals Goethe's own. Ironically Goethe's Faust, his Hamlet, has no personality at all, and is as colorless as Shakespeare himself seems to have chosen to be. Yet nothing could be more colorful than the Second Part of *Faust*, which is peopled by an astonishing array of monsters, grotesque devils and classical ghosts.

A contrast between Shakespeare and Goethe demonstrates that in each—but in very different ways—we can better find the work in the person, than we can discover that banal entity, the person in the work. Goethe to many of his contemporaries, seemed to be a mortal god. Shakespeare, so far as we know, seemed an affable, rather ordinary fellow, who aged early and became somewhat withdrawn. Yet Faust, though Mephistopheles battles for his soul, is hardly worth the trouble unless you take him as an idea and not as a person. Hamlet is nearly every-idea-in-one, but he is precisely a personality and a person.

Would Hamlet be so astonishingly persuasive if his father's ghost did not haunt him? Falstaff is more alive than Prince Hal, who says that the devil haunts him in the shape of an old fat man. Three years before composing the final *Hamlet*, Shakespeare invented Falstaff, who then never ceased to haunt his creator. Falstaff and Hamlet may be said to best represent the work in the writer, because their influence upon Shakespeare was prodigious. W.H. Auden accurately observed that Falstaff possesses infinite energy: never tired, never bored, and absolutely both witty and happy until Hal's rejection destroys him. Hamlet too has infinite energy, but in him it is more curse than blessing.

Falstaff and Hamlet can be said to occupy the roles in Shakespeare's invented world that Sancho Panza and Don Quixote possess in Cervantes's. Shakespeare's plays from 1610 on (starting with *Twelfth Night*) are thus analogous to the Second Part of Cervantes's epic novel. Sancho and the Don overtly jostle Cervantes for authorship in the Second Part, even as Cervantes battles against the impostor who has pirated a continuation of his work. As a dramatist, Shakespeare manifests the work in the writer more indirectly. Falstaff's prose genius is revived in the scapegoating of Malvolio by Maria and Sir Toby Belch, while Falstaff's darker insights are developed by Feste's melancholic wit. Hamlet's intellectual resourcefulness, already deadly, becomes poisonous in Iago and in Edmund. Yet we have not crossed into the deeper abysses of the work in the writer in later Shakespeare.

No fictive character, before or since, is Falstaff's equal in self-trust. Sir John, whose delight in himself is contagious, has total confidence both in his self-awareness and in the resources of his language. Hamlet, whose self is as strong, and whose language is as copious, nevertheless distrusts both the self and language. Later Shakespeare is, as it were, much under the influence both of Falstaff and of Hamlet, but they tug him in opposite directions. Shakespeare's own copiousness of language is well-nigh incredible: a vocabulary in excess of twenty-one thousand words, almost eighteen hundred of which he coined himself. And of his word-hoard, nearly half are used only once each, as though the perfect setting for each had been found, and need not be repeated. Love for language and faith in language are Falstaffian attributes. Hamlet will darken both that love and that faith in Shakespeare, and perhaps the Sonnets can best be read as Falstaff and Hamlet counterpointing against one another.

Can we surmise how aware Shakespeare was of Falstaff and Hamlet, once they had played themselves into existence? *Henry IV, Part I* appeared in six quarto editions during Shakespeare's lifetime; *Hamlet* possibly had four. Falstaff and Hamlet were played again and again at the Globe, but Shakespeare knew also that they were being read, and he must have had contact with some of those readers. What would it have been like to discuss Falstaff or Hamlet with one of their early readers (presumably also part of their audience at the Globe), if you were the creator of such demiurges? The question would seem nonsensical to most Shakespeare scholars, but then these days they tend to be either ideologues or moldy figs. How can we recover the uncanniness of Falstaff and of Hamlet, when they now have become so familiar?

A writer's influence upon himself is an unexplored problem in criticism, but such an influence is never free from anxieties. The biocritical problem (which this series attempts to explore) can be divided into two areas, difficult to disengage fully. Accomplished works affect the author's life, and also affect her subsequent writings. It is simpler for me to surmise the effect of *Mrs. Dalloway* and *To the Lighthouse* upon Woolf's late *Between the Acts*, than it is to relate Clarissa Dalloway's suicide and Lily Briscoe's capable endurance in art to the tragic death and complex life of Virginia Woolf.

There are writers whose lives were so vivid that they seem sometimes to obscure the literary achievement: Byron, Wilde, Malraux, Hemingway. But most major Western writers do not live that exuberantly, and the greatest of all, Shakespeare, sometimes appears to have adopted the personal mask of colorlessness. And yet there are heroes of literature who struggled titanically with their own eras—Tolstoy, Milton, Victor Hugo—who nevertheless matter more for their works than their lives.

There are great figures—Emily Dickinson, Wallace Stevens, Willa Cather—who seem to have had so little of the full intensity of life when compared to the vitality of their work, that we might almost speak of the work in the work, rather than even of the work in a person. Emily Brontë might well be the extreme instance of such a visionary, surpassing William Blake in that one regard.

I conclude this general introduction to a series of literary bio-critiques by stating a tentative formula or principle for gauging the many ways in which the work influences the person and her subsequent, later work. Our influence upon ourselves is always related to the Shakespearean invention of self-overhearing, which I have written about in several other contexts. Life, as well as poetry and prose, is overheard rather than simply heard. The writer listens to herself as though she were somebody else, and the will to change begins to operate. The forces that live in us include the prior work we have done, and the dreams and waking visions that evade our dismissals.

HAROLD BLOOM

Introduction

Scott Fitzgerald's favorite poet was John Keats. An incisive reader, Fitzgerald understood Keats very well, and adapted the work of the Romantic poet skillfully, as in the scene where Gatsby piles up his beautiful shirts for the admiring Daisy, precisely as Porphyro heaps mounds of dainties and sweetmeats for his Madeline in *The Eve of St. Agnes.* The saddest and most intricate employment of Keats by Fitzgerald is in the title of his most ambitious novel, *Tender Is the Night* (1934). Six years before, Fitzgerald had published his masterpiece, *The Great Gatsby*, and six years later, in 1940, he died of an alcohol-induced heart attack, aged 46.

Tender Is the Night has its virtues, and its admirers, but does not sustain rereading, as *Gatsby* does. Its despair, and knowing failure, are prefigured in the Keatsian title, taken from the fourth stanza of the "Ode to a Nightingale." The third stanza sets the context from which the fourth seeks flight:

> Fade far away, dissolve, and quite forget
> What thou among the leaves hast never known,
> The weariness, the fever, and the fret
> Here, where men sit and hear each other groan;
> Where palsy shakes a few, sad, last grey hairs,
> Where youth grows pale, and spectre-thin, and dies;
> Where but to think is to be full of sorrow
>   And leaden-eyed despairs,
> Where Beauty cannot keep her lustrous eyes,
>   Or new Love pine at them beyond tomorrow.

1

That is the cosmos of Scott Fitzgerald in his late thirties, and of Dick Diver in *Tender Is the Night*. The beautiful fourth stanza takes Keats (and Fitzgerald, and Diver) out of the world of aging and of faithless love and into a realm of surmise:

> Away! away! for I will fly to thee,
>   Not charioted by Bacchus and his pards,
> But on the viewless wings of Poesy,
>   Though the dull brain perplexes and retards:
> Already with thee! tender is the night,
>   And haply the Queen-Moon is on her throne,
>   Clustered around by all her starry Fays;
>   But here there is no light,
> Save what from heaven is with the breezes blown
>   Through verdurous glooms and winding mossy ways.

Bacchus, god of alcohol, is abandoned for poetic vision: "Though the dull brain perplexes and retards," intellectually doubting the imagination. And suddenly, Keats takes flight and joins the nightingale's song, in the darkness:

> Already with thee! tender is the night . . .

We are in that place Dick Diver sought (and found) in his idealized marriage to Nicole, which destroyed him, slowly but inexorably. "Tender is the night" *within* the song of the nightingale, but, with Keats, Fitzgerald the Diver emerges from that song to ask himself the ultimate question of those failed by their vision:

> Forlorn! the very word is like a bell
> To toll me back from thee to my sole self!
> Adieu! the fancy cannot cheat so well
>   As she is famed to do, deceiving elf.
> Adieu! adieu! thy plaintive anthem fades
>   Past the near meadows, over the still stream,
>   Up the hill-side; and now 'tis buried deep
>   In the next valley-glades:
> Was it a vision, or a waking dream?
>   Fled is that music: – Do I wake or sleep?

The most eloquent paragraph in *Tender Is the Night* concludes the novel:

After that he didn't ask for the children to be sent to America and didn't answer when Nicole wrote asking him if he needed money. In the last letter she had from him he told her that he was practicing in Geneva, New York, and she got the impression that he had settled down with some one to keep house for him. She looked up Geneva in an atlas and found it was in the heart of the Finger Lakes Section and considered a pleasant place. Perhaps, so she liked to think, his career was biding its time, again like Grant's in Galena; his latest note was post-marked from Hornell, New York, which is some distance from Geneva and a very small town; in any case he is almost certainly in that section of the country, in one town or another.

Dick Diver fades out like Lydgate in George Eliot's *Middlemarch*: a failure in the provinces. Scott Fitzgerald, in his six remaining years, went out rather more spectacularly as a Hollywood alcoholic screenwriter, archetype of *The Crack-Up*, the title of a collection of posthumously collected pieces. "In the real Dark Night of the Soul it is always four-o-clock in the morning" was his memorable, pragmatic self-epitaph.

The malign influence of Fitzgerald's life upon his work is fabled, perhaps too much so. One wonders about the effect of the great work, *The Great Gatsby*, upon the writer from the age of thirty on, when the novel was published. The influence of *The Bridge* (1930) upon Hart Crane in his two remaining years was destructive, partly because of the literary world's myth that such a superb visionary epic was a "failure." But Crane might have been no better served had *The Bridge* been the "success" that *The Great Gatsby* was. Alcoholic, like Fitzgerald, Crane leaped to his Caribbean death in 1932 partly because he was convinced that his poetic gifts had failed, but "The Broken Tower" shows how tragically mistaken he was.

Scott Fitzgerald wrote his "The Broken Tower" in the best of his stories, "Babylon Revisited" (1931), where the final paragraph prefigures the pathos of Dick Diver's defeat:

He would come back some day; they couldn't make him pay forever. But he wanted his child, and nothing was much good now, beside the fact. He wasn't young any more, with a lot of nice thoughts and dreams to have by himself. He was absolutely sure Helen wouldn't have wanted him to be so alone.

The reverberating sentence there is almost a palinode in relation to Jay Gatsby's American Dream:

He wasn't young any more, with a lot of nice thoughts and dreams to have by himself.

NORMA JEAN LUTZ

Biography of F. Scott Fitzgerald

The Fairytale Begins

On a quiet September day in St. Paul, Minnesota—still a relatively small town in the year 1919—a slender, fair-haired young man bursts out of the front door of the three-story stone house at 599 Summit Avenue. His behavior is startling for this respectable upper-class neighborhood replete with stately, gingerbread-trimmed Victorian homes. In his hand he's waving a sheet of paper—a letter—and he's shouting to passersby the wonderful news he's just received. His first novel, *This Side of Paradise*, has been accepted by a New York publisher, and his joy knows no bounds.

Twenty-three-year-old F. Scott Fitzgerald had gambled everything on this one novel, and his first taste of success was sweet. Two months earlier, July 4th to be exact, Fitzgerald had quit his job writing ads in New York City and returned to his hometown of St. Paul. There he cloistered himself in a small stuffy third-floor room, and pressed on to finish the novel. Through the hot summer days, his pen scratched out page after page.

The move home to live with his parents was something of a come-down for this rather vain young man. He was home, after all, pursuing a goal that both of his parents disagreed with. His mother had hoped Scott would become a career soldier, and his father wanted him to become a businessman. Despite their disapproval, neither forbade him to return.

By this age, Fitzgerald had already experienced his share of dashed dreams and unfortunate failures, but this time was different. This time there was more at stake. This time there was a girl waiting. An important, beautiful girl named Zelda waited for her successful suitor in the deep south of Montgomery, Alabama.

Fitzgerald's engagement to Zelda had been an on-again, off-again affair. She was determined to wait for the person who could support her in the manner to which she was accustomed, while Fitzgerald tried to prove that he was that person. Her dreams included not only money but excitement as well, and Fitzgerald's 90-dollar-a-month job at Barron Collier Advertising Agency did not fit these plans. The unfinished novel held Fitzgerald's last thread of hope for winning Zelda's affections.

Fitzgerald's book had been accepted at Scribner & Sons publishing company, and his editor, the famous Maxwell Perkins, took quite a risk on this new unknown writer. The turnaround on the manuscript was surprisingly quick, especially for that day and time. Fitzgerald had dropped his manuscript into the mail on September 4, and the good news had arrived before the month was over.

Writing back to Perkins, young Fitzgerald's excitement jumped off the page: "Of course I was delighted to get your letter, and I've been in a sort of trance all day; not that I doubted you'd take it but at last I have something to show people."

"Showing people," had always been important to F. Scott Fitzgerald.

Perkins, one of the great American editors of his era, was no stranger to Fitzgerald's work. In August 1918, he had rejected Fitzgerald's earlier full-length novel attempt entitled *The Romantic Egotist*. The writing was an account of his years in prep school and college. While not a very good novel, the writing style caught Perkins's attention and he encouraged Fitzgerald to keep on trying. Maxwell Perkins would remain F. Scott Fitzgerald's sole editor and close friend for the duration of his career.

The sale of his first novel brought about revolutionary changes in Fitzgerald's life. He lost no time in returning to New York City, moving out of his tiny apartment in the Bronx to the fashionable Knickerbocker Hotel in Manhattan. News of his success convinced magazine editors to purchase his stories. Harold Ober of Paul R. Reynolds and Son Literary Agency became Fitzgerald's agent. Ober not only negotiated a sale of a short story to *The Saturday Evening Post* for $400, he sold one of Fitzgerald's short stories to Metro-Goldwyn-Mayer for the movies.

Flushed with pride and excitement, Fitzgerald instinctively turned to drink to celebrate. Unfortunately, this instinct would prove to be his eventual downfall.

In January 1920, buoyed by success, Fitzgerald visited Montgomery and easily convinced Zelda to become his wife. His friends warned him that she was much too ambitious and headstrong for him, but he did not listen. She was the prize he was after and he felt he would die if he did not have her.

The engagement was on again and was announced in Montgomery social circles in March. Zelda wrote Scott with all the confidence of youth, "... we're going to marry and live happily ever afterward ..."

The two were married in the rectory of St. Patrick's Cathedral in New York City, April 3, 1920, with eight people in attendance.

The first edition of Fitzgerald's novel had already sold out, and now the prince had married his princess. "Happily ever after" seemed a foregone conclusion. Instead, the fairytale turned into a series of tragedies from which the couple would never recover.

DEVELOPING A "TWO CYLINDER INFERIORITY COMPLEX"

F. Scott Fitzgerald said of his origins, "I am half black Irish and half old American stock.... The black Irish half of the family had the money and looked down upon the Maryland side.... So being born in that atmosphere of crack, wise crack and countercrack I developed a two cylinder inferiority complex."

F. Scott Fitzgerald's mother, Mary "Mollie" McQuillan, came from a well-to-do merchant family from the upper strata of St. Paul society. Her father, Philip McQuillan, came to America from Ireland with only a few dollars in his pocket, but turned his dollars into a fortune in the wholesale grocery business. Even though he died at a young age, Philip left his widow and four children, of which Mollie was the eldest, an inheritance that provided many years of financial security. The McQuillan mansion proudly stood on Summit Avenue, one of the most respected streets to live on during St. Paul's "golden years," when social position meant a great deal.

Mollie grew to be a plain but eccentric woman who cared little about her appearance—a trait that later became a source of embarrassment to her son. However, her stubborn determination often got her what she wanted in life.

In stark contrast to the bold, moneyed, Irish McQuillan family was Scott's father, the quiet, mannerly Edward Fitzgerald. Edward conveyed the stereotype of the typical Southern gentleman, dapper and distinguished looking with a gentle disposition. The Fitzgerald side of the family traced its roots back to the American Revolution. Francis Scott Key, author of the national anthem, was a distant cousin of Edward's mother.

The coming together of this unlikely couple—Southern gentleman Edward Fitzgerald, and the outspoken, strong-willed Mollie McQuillan—set the sometimes tragic stage for the life of their son Francis Scott Key Fitzgerald, who was born September 24, 1896.

Prior to Scott's birth, Mollie had suffered two miscarriages, and the death of a third child in infancy. By the time Scott arrived, his mother was 30, and his father was 37. Their advanced age coupled with the grief of their previous losses encouraged them to dote on and pamper young Scott.

Scott's formative years were spent in endless moves. At the time of his birth, Edward owned a furniture store in St. Paul. When this business failed, he found a job with Procter and Gamble, which meant uprooting the family and moving to Buffalo, New York. In New York, the family residence switched back and forth between Buffalo and Syracuse, and also from neighborhood to neighborhood within each city.

In the midst of such mobility, Scott created a more stable fantasy world. He remembers having the ability to tell "enormous lies to older people." Books that he read and plays that he watched at the theater added fuel to the fire of this powerful imagination. At age 10, he would come home from a Saturday afternoon at the theater and dress up in costume and put on his own plays. When involving other children in his drama, he made sure he was always the central character.

Molly indulged her son in his grandiosity, often agreeing that he should be the center of attention. She impressed upon him that he was special and that he was a born leader. Seldom was he disciplined by either parent. In 1900, Scott was sent off to grammar school, but because he cried he was taken out after one morning. Later he convinced his parents that he could bear only half days of school.

A sister, Annabel, arrived in 1901. Little about her is known. The pampered young Scott never seemed to be upstaged by the arrival of this younger sibling.

In March 1908, Edward lost his job. Fearful that they would go to the poorhouse, Scott realized with a jolt that money was vitally important. An incessant fear of poverty, exaggerated by his own inability to handle money, would haunt him in the years to come.

There were few options open to the family but to pack up and return to St. Paul, where the security of the McQuillan money would take care of them. Now viewed as a failure, Scott's father became a nonentity whose opinions mattered very little.

While the McQuillan money made the family comfortable, they were by no means rich. The air of family superiority created by Scott's mother forced them to act the part regardless of the actual circumstances. After several moves within the city of St. Paul, the family settled into a house down Summit Avenue from the McQuillan mansion, at a juncture where the nicer neighborhood merged with one of a lesser social standing.

Here Scott spent his adolescent years putting on plays, collecting stamps and cigar bands, writing stories, and playing on the neighborhood football team. Although small for his age, Scott believed that, much like in the popular novels he'd read, enough pluck and determination would allow him to excel in sports and become the hero.

Unfortunately, his mother's coddling and his own need to excel at everything made Scott an unpopular student when he enrolled in St. Paul Academy in September 1908. He quickly became the star of the school debating team and often led the clubs that he organized. His relentless pursuit of athletic prowess continued as he broke a rib playing football and never made it past the third team in baseball. To his credit, Scott pursued everything with an unusual tenacity.

Off the field and out of the classroom, Scott wrote plays and stories, one of which was published in the St. Paul Academy school magazine, *Now and Then*. Scott's writing also found its way into his own personal journal, which he called his "Thoughtbook." Here he recorded school activities, analyzed his fellow classmates, and poured out his own emotions.

At the local dancing school, where the children came decked out in their finery, Scott's good looks and gracious manner won the attention of a pretty girl named Kitty Williams. The boys, on the other hand, did not like his aggressive personality. His nonstop talking prompted an article in the school paper to ask if someone would "poison Scotty or find some means to shut his mouth."

In spite of Scott's apparent intelligence, his grades suffered during his two years at St. Paul Academy. He was an easily distracted student who found clubs, games, dancing, and writing to be much more fun than lessons. Classroom work bored him, so he penned stories in the back of textbooks and in the margins of his math papers.

Rather than addressing the problem, his parents felt the solution would be to send him to an East coast boarding school. This further allowed Scott to shirk responsibility and avoid the consequences of his actions—a pattern that would follow him into adulthood.

The Fitzgeralds chose the Newman School, a Catholic preparatory school just outside Hackensack, New Jersey, only 40 minutes from New York City. His parents reasoned that the smaller student body of only 60 students would offer Scott the personal attention he deserved.

The very thought of an Eastern boarding school thrilled Scott. All upstanding St. Paul families sent their sons to the East for culture and for training. He saw the change as a fresh opportunity to become popular and to fulfill his long-standing dream of becoming the athletic hero.

Before leaving for Newman in 1911, Fitzgerald filled his Thoughtbook with personal inventories. He saw himself as gifted with superior mental abilities, but mechanically inferior. He knew he was handsome and charming and poised, while at the same time he admitted to being somewhat fresh and moody. On top of everything, he admitted he was selfish. With this in mind, he hit the Newman campus with a powerful drive and enthusiasm to succeed.

The prep school's campus fit the image of Fitzgerald's dreams: old ivy-covered buildings, neat rows of cottages as student dorms, plus gymnasiums and athletic fields. Unfortunately, Fitzgerald brought his same obnoxious temperament to bear on his new peers. He quickly became the most unpopular boy at the school. The other boys saw him as too pretty, in addition to being loud and brash. He arrived late for classes and failed to hand in assignments, habits that offended the more responsible students.

In boarding school life, socioeconomic class often is given inflated importance. It was under such conditions that Fitzgerald experienced his first vivid impression of being the poor boy among the rich. It was a feeling he did not like and one he would write about in later years. The need for money in order to achieve social standing became greatly exaggerated in his mind.

However, weekend trips to visit the theater in New York City became one bright spot in Fitzgerald's life. Drama had long been a source of fascination for him, but the touring groups he'd seen in St. Paul now paled in comparison to the thrill and excitement of Broadway. The popular musical comedies of the day inspired an eager Fitzgerald to intently study the works of Gilbert and Sullivan, as he filled notebooks with his own musical comedy renditions.

When Fitzgerald lost the privilege of these weekend trips because of his poor grades, he was surprised and crushed. It was the first time in his life he was held accountable for his actions.

During the summer between his two years at Newman, Fitzgerald wrote plays and worked with a St. Paul drama group, drawing his inspiration from Broadway.

His second year at Newman was better. Once again, he used his Thoughtbook to take stock of things, and he made a concerted effort to become more thoughtful of others and less selfish. Fitzgerald's long-standing dream to make the football team came true at last, and he succeeded in becoming the star of one Newman game. Fitzgerald's other successes, almost all extracurricular, included obtaining a position as editor of the *Newman News*, winning a part in a school play, and being awarded a prize for his performance in various elocution contests.

The most significant event of this period was Fitzgerald's acquaintance with Father Sigourney Fay, a Newman trustee. As a wealthy man of good taste and cultivation—who possessed the ability to communicate with young people—Father Fay introduced Fitzgerald to the world of sophisticated upper-class Eastern Catholics. This luxurious world seemed far removed from the straitlaced Catholics of his St. Paul childhood.

Father Fay evidently detected the seeds of genius in young Fitzgerald and invested time in his pupil's life. Their long talks were usually centered on the beauties and intricacies of literature. As a needed father figure, Father Fay also gave wise counsel. He would later be immortalized in Fitzgerald's novel *This Side of Paradise*, where he appeared in the novel as Father Darcy. The book was dedicated to Father Fay.

The two maintained a close friendship even after Fitzgerald left Newman. Upon Father Fay's death in 1919, Fitzgerald wrote to a friend, "I can't realize that he has gone. That all of us who loved him have lost him forever and that that side of life is over, the great warmth and atmosphere that he could cast over youth—the perfect understanding."

Soon Fitzgerald began to consider different colleges. For quite some time, he had admired Princeton. Fitzgerald could relate to their underdog status, as they would barely miss winning the football championships. Furthermore, Princeton had a theatrical group called the Triangle Club, a feature that appealed to the aspiring dramatist in Fitzgerald. Finally, in the spring of his senior year, he discovered a musical comedy score written by the Triangle Club—a discovery that convinced him Princeton was the school he should attend.

The desire to attend Princeton was easy enough; it was getting in that would prove to be the challenge. Once again, his poor study habits came back to haunt him. After failing the entrance exam in the spring of 1913, he was told to study during the summer and take a makeup exam in the fall.

Determined, Fitzgerald spent long hours studying throughout the hot summer days back home in St. Paul. He also found time to work with the local drama group, writing a play entitled *The Coward*, which met with a degree of success. The local papers were already making Scott somewhat of a local celebrity and pointed to him as a young man filled with promise—one to be closely watched.

When fall arrived, Fitzgerald left for Princeton, where he took the makeup exam and failed once again. His scores were high enough to allow him to appeal the case. Further determined, Fitzgerald's acceptance to his coveted school bordered on obsession, and his grandiosity spurred him on.

With his usual charm he spoke to the officials, outlining his many talents and abilities, eventually convincing them that he would be a great student for the school. The day of the appeal was September 24, his 17th birthday. Shamelessly Fitzgerald used that ploy to his advantage, saying that a rejection on his birthday would be cruel.

The officials relented. Triumphant and confident, he sent his mother this telegram: "ADMITTED SEND FOOTBALL PADS AND SHOES IMMEDIATELY PLEASE WAIT TRUNK."

STRUGGLES AND TRIUMPHS AT PRINCETON

When F. Scott Fitzgerald arrived at Princeton in the fall of 1913, football was the defining factor for social acceptance. Having never lost his desire to be the little guy who wins against all odds, he went out for the team. To his great disappointment, his 135-pound, five-foot-seven-inch frame couldn't make the grade. He was out the first day, shattering forever his lifelong dream of being the acclaimed football hero.

Princeton, a school steeped in wealthy conservatism, was home to young eastern aristocrats. Again Fitzgerald was an outsider—he was neither wealthy nor an easterner. Refusing to accept this role Fitzgerald quickly became obsessed with gaining the acceptance of his peers.

Delighted by the rules for freshmen, from curfew to dress codes to being prohibited to smoke a pipe, Fitzgerald felt these were the true marks of being a Princeton man. He eagerly wore his black freshman skullcap, cuffless trousers, and stiff-collared shirts. The Princeton campus not only filled him with pride, but he reveled in its elegant beauty:

> Two tall spires and then suddenly all around you spreads out the loveliest riot of Gothic architecture in America, battlement linked on to battlement, hall to hall; arch-broken, vine-covered—luxuriant and lovely over two square miles of green grass. Here is no monotony, no feeling that it was all built yesterday at the whim of last week's millionaire ...

Fitzgerald felt that his years at Princeton would be critical. He was convinced that his future would rise or fall on what happened in this time and place. It became imperative that he not only be accepted, but also that he reign in a secure position of leadership.

Since football had been eliminated, he quickly sought alternative avenues to become the big man on campus. First and foremost, he looked to the Triangle Club, which had been established years earlier by southern author, Booth Tarkington. The Triangle Club not only wrote and put on reviews, it also toured the United States with its productions. This gave the students nationwide recognition—an opportunity that appealed to Scott.

After the Triangle Club, there were the literary publications, such as the newspaper, *The Princetonian*, and a humor sheet called *The Tiger*, both of which would later publish Fitzgerald's writings. Finally he would turn to the clubs that offered the highest mark of social standing.

During his first semester, Scott flooded *The Tiger* with submissions until he was finally published. Breaking into the Triangle Club proved more difficult. After his submissions were turned down, he agreed to work on stage lighting—anything to make himself useful and to be in the presence of the legitimate members.

Repeating his Newman performance, Fitzgerald poured his time and energy into extracurricular activities, at the expense of his studies. By the time semester break rolled around, he was close to flunking out. Fortunately, with a concerted effort, he was able to pull his grades up the following spring. This effort was further complicated by his near-feverish work on an entry for the annual competition for an original musical comedy for the Triangle Club.

With the Triangle Club's acceptance of his book and lyrics for the final competition, Fitzgerald was elated and confident that his road to fame was neatly paved. Furthermore, his work would now be exposed nationwide.

As he reviewed his freshman year, Fitzgerald felt he'd been successful. His success was furthered when he found an entrée into the upper class as Father Fay invited Fitzgerald to his mother's home in New Jersey for a visit. There Fitzgerald intermingled with the cultivated and the refined. Even though he felt outclassed, he was confident he would find his way as a legitimate part of high society.

Of the close friends that Scott made that first year, John Peale Bishop made the greatest impression. Bishop was four years older, having been kept out of school due to a childhood illness. Bishop, who went on to become an essayist and poet, spent hours with Fitzgerald in deep conversations on literature, about which Bishop was somewhat of an expert.

Low grades notwithstanding, Scott returned home to St. Paul pleased and proud of his many accomplishments. He spent the summer between his freshman and sophomore years at White Bear Yacht Club where he wrote, produced, and directed yet another successful play for the local drama group. Studying also filled his hours, as he crammed to make up the courses he had failed.

Upon his return to Princeton in the fall of 1914, he found his greatest dream had come true. His play *Fie!Fie!Fi-Fi!* had been accepted by the Triangle Club. Unfortunately, Fitzgerald's elation was dampened when the Faculty Committee decided that due to his low grades, Fitzgerald would be ineligible to either act in the play or travel with the troupe. Once again, he suffered failure as a result of his own actions. He remained resentful for years to come.

Almost immediately, wrote a story about his experience entitled "The Spire and the Gargoyle." In the story, the spire represents the talented student striving for high-minded success. The gargoyle is the narrow-minded instructor who can deprive that student of honors because of academic failure. The story was published in February 1917, in Princeton's *Nassau Literary Magazine.*

True to his indomitable spirit, Fitzgerald plunged in to do everything possible to help with the production, to the point of supervising the smallest details. The show was a hit, with the audience cheering Fitzgerald's lyrics.

At Christmas break, the troupe left to go on tour, and Fitzgerald returned to St. Paul. His anger over not being able to tour was tempered by the excellent reviews of the show coming in from around the country. The critic in the *Louisville Post* wrote, "The lyrics of the songs were written by F. S. Fitzgerald, who could take his place right now with the brightest writers of witty lyrics in America."

As fortune would have it, had Fitzgerald traveled with the touring group that Christmas vacation, he would not have met the first true love of his life. Ginevra King was a 16-year-old, doe-eyed beauty who attended Westover School in Chicago, and she'd come to St. Paul to visit her school roommate, Marie "Midge" Hersey. Midge and Scott had grown up together and Midge wanted Ginevra to meet the town's greatest celebrity, F. Scott Fitzgerald.

When the two were introduced at the St. Paul Country Club on January 2, Fitzgerald was smitten. He was impressed not only by her stunning beauty, but also by her charm and the relative ease with which she moved among the rich.

In Ginevra, Fitzgerald discovered his dream girl—a girl to whom he could become totally devoted. And over all the other available men who were at the dance, she chose him. For a young man who struggled with shaky self-esteem and a longing to be accepted, this was a heady experience.

Their time together was short, as both had to return to school. In his letters to her, Fitzgerald wrote of his commitment to her. However, when she reciprocated, he struggled to believe her. Jealousy surfaced in many of his letters.

When he visited her at Westover they were closely supervised by a chaperone. Nevertheless, Ginevra was given enough time with Fitzgerald to be taken by his wit and charm. Later that year, he wanted her to attend the sophomore prom, but since her mother was unable to come along and chaperone, she had to decline the invitation. Fitzgerald took this as a personal affront and became bitter and angry.

It seems odd that Fitzgerald's sense of self-worth should flounder at this time, as things were going well for him at Princeton. At the mid-year test, he passed every class except one. With his privileges returned to him, he bid for entrance into the elite social clubs on campus. Similar to a fraternity, the club was where the student lived, ate, studied, courted his girl, and discussed intellectual subjects with his peers. Fitzgerald was pursued by several of the clubs, and he chose the most prestigious, the Cottage Club.

Membership in the Cottage Club was like the master key that opened doors to further social success. The Triangle Club elected him as its secretary; *The Tiger* elected him to its editorial board; *Nassau Lit* published more and more of his writings, after which he was singled out as a promising up-and-coming young writer. This portion of his sophomore year proved to be the pinnacle of his college career.

His long-standing dream was to eventually become president of the Triangle Club and serve on the Senior Council. In his ebullience over these advances, he once again neglected his studies. At the close of his sophomore year, he failed three more subjects.

In June, Fitzgerald and Ginevra enjoyed a short time together in New York City. There they attended the theater and later danced at the Ritz Roof. During this happy time, they again pledged their love to one another.

During the summer of 1915, Fitzgerald then traveled to Wyoming with a school friend. By the close of summer, his infatuation with Ginevra seemed to have cooled somewhat.

As a big man on campus, Fitzgerald took even more liberties than when he was a freshman, cutting classes and avoiding assignments. Eventually, the same "gargoyles" that barred him from extracurricular activities when he was a sophomore barred him from positions of leadership and any activities outside the classroom.

While Fitzgerald knew it was his fault, such self-awareness did little to temper his anger or bitterness—an anger that only caused his grades suffer further. To Fitzgerald, the essence of school was extracurricular activities and social life. In November he was diagnosed with malaria, relatively common among Princeton students at that time due to the surrounding swampy lands. The next month he decided to take a leave of absence and return home—his sickness served as a good excuse.

The next few months back home in St. Paul were depressing and miserable. His mother, whose eccentric mannerisms had long irritated Scott, was now almost unbearable. Feelings of failure threatened to consume him: "To me college would never be the same. There were to be no badges of pride, no medals, after all. It seemed on one March afternoon that I had lost every single thing I wanted…"

Success at Princeton had held the possibility of wiping out every insecurity that had ever plagued him. Upon his returned to Princeton in the fall of 1916, Fitzgerald learned that he would have to repeat his entire junior year over again. This would move him out of the level of his esteemed peers and classmates. His circle of friends quickly changed during this time. Depressed and deflated, he gravitated toward more serious students who read serious literature and weren't so much affected by social standings. Despite his earlier successes, when Fitzgerald wrote another libretto for the Triangle Club, it was rejected.

At the conclusion of his junior year, Fitzgerald had become disillusioned with formal studies. At that same time, his relationship with Ginevra ended when she announced that she was not ready for a long-term commitment. In keeping with his insecurities, Fitzgerald preferred to believe her reluctance was due to his lack of wealth and prestige. Even after the relationship was over, he would think about her and write about her for years to come. He kept her letters for the rest of his life. Years later, in a letter to his daughter, Scott wrote: "On such paper, but with the Princeton seal, I used to write endless letters throughout sophomore and junior years to Ginevra King of Chicago and Westover.... She was the first girl I ever loved..."

Fitzgerald believed that romantic disappointment left permanent scars, a philosophy that allowed him to nurse old wounds for a very long time.

Meanwhile, the war in Europe demanded everyone's attention in the spring of 1917, even the young men at Princeton. That next summer, surrounded by his more serious friends, they talked of nothing but war and how they would all become heroes—a notion that held great promise for the downtrodden Fitzgerald.

In July, he took the examination for an army commission, which came through in October of his senior year. This gave Fitzgerald a gallant exit from his failures and shortcomings at Princeton. Now before him lay the exciting possibility of becoming a nationally known war hero.

ENTERING THE WAR

Fitzgerald's desire to be a war hero overrode any distaste for war itself. While he scorned the conventional patriotic attitude that swept America at the time, he was far from being a pacifist. His comment was, "I'm too Irish for that."

His first post in Ft. Leavenworth, Kansas, was far removed from the ivy-covered walls of Princeton. He arrived full of pride and ambition, dressed in his custom-made uniform purchased at the fashionable Brooks Brothers of New York. In the barracks with 15 other soldiers, he was thought of as being soft and spoiled. One fellow officer was later quoted as saying Fitzgerald was "the world's worst second lieutenant."

In continuing his writing, Fitzgerald brought along his unfinished novel entitled *The Romantic Egotist*. The weak plot consisted mainly of a first-person account of his years at Newman and Princeton. He'd worked on the novel while at school, during which time he'd asked several others to read it. Father Fay felt it was good enough to be submitted right away. His respected professor, Christian Gauss, was more cautious. Dean Gauss felt it needed extensive revisions. While his professor's comment was disappointing, it may have served as the catalyst to keep Fitzgerald working to prove he could do it.

Fitzgerald felt incredible pressure to finish the novel. In his mind, time was very short. "I had only three months to live—in those days all infantry officers had only three months to live—and I had left no mark on the world."

Fitzgerald wrote during army lectures. That he was repeatedly caught and punished made no difference. In fact, it made his effort all the more heroic. Weekends were the only time he had to devote his complete attention to his project.

Spending long hours in the officers' club amidst the noise and distractions, he continued to write. Each finished chapter was mailed to a typist at Princeton. By the spring of 1918, the manuscript was ready to be submitted to Scribner's. Shortly thereafter, he joined the 45th Infantry Regiment in Camp Taylor, Kentucky, and then traveled on to Camp Gordon, Georgia. The war seemed far off and distant. While waiting for word from the publishers, Fitzgerald became increasingly restless and nervous. Being a well-dressed officer wasn't much of a challenge for such a motivated young man.

In June 1918, Fitzgerald's unit was transferred to Camp Sheridan, located about six miles northeast of Montgomery, Alabama, on Lower Wetumpka Road. In the genteel tradition of Southern hospitality, officers were invited to dances at Montgomery's old country club ballroom, where under the brightly colored Japanese paper lanterns Fitzgerald met the beautiful and popular Zelda Sayre.

Eighteen-year-old Zelda had graduated from high school that spring, where she'd established a wild reputation. In her high school photo she is dressed in a simple middy blouse, while her classmates are clad in their Sunday best. Beneath her photo is the caption, "Why should all life be work when we all can borrow. Let's only think of today and not worry about tomorrow." The words would literally become the motto of Zelda's life.

Born in 1900 in Montgomery, Alabama, she was the sixth and youngest child of Minnie Mochen Sayre and Anthony Dickinson Sayre. Minnie Sayre nursed this last child until she was four years old and, much like Fitzgerald, Zelda was pampered and spoiled.

Zelda's mother has been described as "artistic," "creative," and "theatrical." Neighbors described Mrs. Sayre as being a little odd. There may have been a predisposition to mental illness on the maternal side of Zelda's family tree, indicated by Zelda's maternal grandmother having committed suicide. Her father, a well-respected lawyer and judge in Montgomery, was conservative, emotionally reserved and remote.

At age nine, Zelda began taking ballet lessons. Dance would remain an important part of her life. In addition to dance, her interests were swimming and boys. When she graduated from high school in the spring of 1918, she was voted the prettiest in her class.

When in later years Zelda described her childhood and adolescence she wrote that she was "independent, courageous, without thought for anyone else. I had great confidence in myself, even to the extent of walking by myself against life as it was then. I did not have a single feeling of inferiority, or shyness, or doubts, and no moral principles."

In spite of the fact that she was the daughter of a well-respected judge, her rebelliousness led her to drink and smoke even as a teenager. While she appeared unaccountable and invincible, her actions still fell within the confines of her father's firm hand, and the close quarters of a small community. Later, when those confines were removed, young Zelda found she was very much at a loss.

When wartime Montgomery met with an influx of army officers, Zelda became the center of attention. She enjoyed the officers' company and she enjoyed being a flirt. Young pilots from the flying school took turns buzzing her house until they were ordered to stop.

Having only recently learned of the marriage of Ginevra King, Fitzgerald was ready for Zelda to come into his life. While the two fell quickly in love, theirs was not a quiet, settled relationship. Both agreed that they wanted much out of life, but both wanted to retain their "sovereign rights as individuals." Of the two, Fitzgerald appeared more willing to commit to the relationship, while Zelda hedged, unsure that Fitzgerald would be a suitable provider. She hungered for success, both social and financial, and she was willing to wait for it.

Although Zelda's social standing was much below that of Ginevra's, still Fitzgerald found his old insecurities rising up to plague him. He desperately feared losing Zelda, but hoped the acceptance of his novel would change all that.

The bad news arrived in August. The rejected manuscript arrived in the mail with a request for extensive rewrites. With renewed energies Fitzgerald set about to make the requested revisions. Once again the manuscript was turned down, this time for good. Only one editor at Scribner's had favored accepting the manuscript—his name was Maxwell Perkins, the man who later became Fitzgerald's lifelong editor.

While Fitzgerald's hopes for becoming a successful author had evaporated, his chance to become a war hero finally arrived in October. His division left the South to arrive at Camp Mills in Long Island, New York. He was informed it would be only a matter of days before they left for the front.

During these days of boredom and frustration, Fitzgerald repeatedly got himself into trouble, often a result of his drinking. His future as a writer was in question, as was his relationship with Zelda, and when he could not cope he turned to alcohol. After only a few drinks, Fitzgerald could quickly lose his charm and become argumentative and disagreeable.

At last he found himself on a train headed for Quebec, where he would board ship for Europe and the battlefront. Before they ever arrived in Canada, however, word came that the war was ending. The armistice ending World War I was signed on November 11, 1918. Visions of war medals on his chest went the way of the visions of football trophies. Once again, Fitzgerald was left standing on the outside looking in, as the things he desired most often seemed to be placed just out of his reach.

Fortunately, his unit was shipped back to Montgomery, where he and Zelda were able to spend more time together. She was not yet convinced that he possessed the ability to support her, and at times she purposely spurned his attentions. His only way of handling her rejections was to drink himself into a stupor, firmly establishing alcohol as the crutch that would aid with life's disappointments.

It was also during this time that Father Sigourney Fay died. In a letter to a friend who also knew Father Fay, Fitzgerald wrote, "I've never wanted so much to die in my life.… now my little world made to order has been shattered by the death of one man."

Immediately upon his discharge in February 1919, Fitzgerald returned to New York to seek his fortune. He applied for a job as a reporter with every newspaper in the city, showing samples of his work from his college days. He was turned down by all of them. It was a puzzle he could never fully understand. Later he would write that it was as though "they decided definitely and irrevocably by the sound of my name on a calling card that I was absolutely unfitted to be a reporter."

Eventually Fitzgerald found a menial position with Barron Collier Advertising Agency, writing slogans for trolley car ads. In his spare time he wrote short stories at a fevered pitch. The walls of his small stuffy apartment in the Bronx were lined with the many rejection slips he received. His wealthy buddies from Princeton, meanwhile, feasted on the good life. The contrast bothered Fitzgerald more than it ever had before:

> As I hovered ghost-like in the Plaza Red Room of a Saturday afternoon, or went to lush and liquid garden parties in the East Sixties or tippled with Princetonians in the Biltmore Bar I was

haunted always by my other life—my drab room in the Bronx, my square foot of the subway, my fixation upon the day's letter from Alabama—would it come and what would it say?—my shabby suits, my poverty, and love. While my friends were launching decently into life I had muscled my inadequate bark into midstream.

Back in Alabama, Zelda was weary of waiting. She was quite sure she would never make it as the wife of a struggling writer, and she made no secret of her longing for glamour and excitement. Fitzgerald's first sale of a short story to a magazine called *The Smart Set* was not sufficient to convince Zelda otherwise.

That summer, Fitzgerald traveled to Montgomery to try to secure their relationship. He pleaded with Zelda to commit to marry him; she refused. After a noisy argument, Zelda broke off the engagement. Despondent and heartbroken, he returned to New York. His mood was described in a letter to a friend: "I've done my best and I've failed. It's a great tragedy to me and I feel I have very little left to live for.... Unless someday she will marry me I will never marry."

His depression led to weeks of drinking. However, when he emerged from the drinking bout, he remembered that he still had his writing. In a nihilistic frenzy, he quit his job and returned to St. Paul, where his second novel was completed and then accepted.

Christening the Jazz Age

This Side of Paradise took the country by storm. While the people at Scribner's informed Fitzgerald that most new authors do well to sell 5,000 copies, he told them he was sure it would sell at least 20,000. He was right. The book both shocked and amused the critics and the public; reviewers raved over it. *The New York Times* wrote, "The glorious spirit of abounding youth glows throughout this fascinating tale."

On this success, Zelda finally agreed to marry Scott. *This Side of Paradise* exposed the follies of the younger generation—and the well-dressed, handsome Fitzgerald, accompanied by his lovely wife, was the perfect representative to ring in this fresh new era. The couple played their parts with gusto.

Success came at Scott and Zelda like a tidal wave, and they attempted to ride the crest as long as it lasted. The couple felt it was their duty to fulfill a certain flamboyant role to please their fans and admirers. (Although in later years, Scott would write that he had been "pushed into the position" of being a spokesman for his time.)

The 1920s marked the advent of extreme changes in society. The nation had been rocked by a world war that had been terribly frightening and serious. In stark contrast, it was now time to forget and have fun.

Women came out of their ankle-length, dark, heavy dresses and wore shortened, gauzy-thin sleeveless frocks. Applying heavy makeup, bobbing their hair, drinking and smoking, they were called "flappers." Flappers lived in an era when they had the privacy of an automobile for courting purposes, something their mothers and grandmothers could never have imagined. Radio was born, bringing on a new level of information and entertainment to every person, not just the elite or the educated.

The Fitzgeralds were most certainly a part of ushering in the "jazz age"—a term that Scott himself coined. In his essay, *Early Success*, Fitzgerald described the times: "The uncertainties of 1919 were over.... America was going on the greatest, gaudiest spree in history and there was going to be plenty to tell about it. The whole golden boom was in the air…"

Following their wedding, the Fitzgeralds lived a wild life in New York City, hopping from party to party and exhibiting antics befitting a pair of unruly adolescents. In the Knickerbocker Hotel, Scott threw $20 and $50 bills around like so much confetti. Zelda jumped into the fountain at Union Square fully clothed. They did handstands in hotel lobbies, rode atop a taxicab down Fifth Avenue late at night, and went whirling about in a revolving door for half an hour. At the theater they laughed at all the wrong places just to get attention. Zelda danced on restaurant tabletops while Scott got falling-down drunk.

Newspaper reporters followed them about, asking their opinions about everything from politics to how to handle finances, then surprised the couple by actually quoting them in the media. Articles about Scott and Zelda appeared in the daily papers and in the popular magazines of the day.

In the midst of the fun and games of that first year of marriage, Fitzgerald managed to write and sell 18 short stories, the prices of which rose right along with his fame. By the close of 1920, he had earned $18,000 (more than he'd ever earned in his life) and yet was $1,600 in debt and had no savings. In nearly every letter to Max Perkins he asked for an advance on future earnings, another habit that dogged him for a lifetime

The young couple became like shooting stars—rising fast, rising bright, and burning out quickly. They grew tired of their wild lives. Beneath the bravado, Zelda was fearful of the big city and Scott was lost and confused about who he was. Zelda's role as the beautiful, confident, daring wife of the handsome, successful young author caused her immense inner pain that would not be revealed until years afterward.

They searched for ways to sustain the ecstatic intoxicated rush that came with this initial wave of success. Much like a married woman who constantly longs to remain a bride, it was an exercise in futility.

In the spring of 1921, they decided to move to Westport, Connecticut, on Long Island Sound. It was an honest endeavor to bring an element of quiet and order to their hectic lives. However, the parties seemed to follow them wherever they went, and the money disappeared just as quickly.

In order to keep the money flowing, Fitzgerald ceased work on his next novel to hurriedly turn out a series of short stories. The volume entitled *Flappers and Philosophers* was published five months after the successful *This Side of Paradise* had hit the stores. This time, reviewers weren't quite as kind, but that was no deterrent. The negative reactions only drove Fitzgerald to work harder on his novel, *The Beautiful and Damned*. By the middle of August, he was promising Max Perkins that it would be finished in November.

While her husband was working furiously on his novel, Zelda was bored and weary of living so far from the glitter of New York. She had not been, and would never be, a contented housewife. The couple began to quarrel loudly and dramatically. By fall they gave up country living and moved to a small apartment near the fashionable Plaza Hotel in the Central Park area.

By the end of December, Fitzgerald was deeper in debt than ever and the novel was still not completed. He'd been paid an advance on a short story and found himself unable to even begin. Frightening as these problems were, they vanished in the spring when Fitzgerald was paid $7,000 for the serialization rights by a magazine. The Fitzgeralds took the money and booked passage on a steamer to Europe.

Their trip was short, beginning in England and traveling on to France and then to Italy. While in England, Fitzgerald met John Galsworthy, another Scribner author whose writing Fitzgerald had admired. This opened doors for Scott and Zelda to meet a number of "important" and noted people.

However, once again the Fitzgeralds became bored quickly. Scott supposed it was because they didn't know anyone. Unfortunately, Italy didn't prove to be much better. Traveling together without an entourage along for excitement left them empty and searching.

Since Zelda was pregnant, they returned to America and tried to decide where to settle until the baby was born. In late July 1921, they traveled to Zelda's home in Alabama, but wavered in their decision whether to remain there or move to St. Paul. Eventually, St. Paul won out. It had already been settled that their baby would not be born in New York City. "It was typical of our precarious position in New York that when our child was to be born we played safe and went home to St. Paul—it seemed inappropriate to bring a baby into all that glamour and loneliness."

Regardless of the hero's welcome he received in St. Paul, Fitzgerald quickly became depressed and restless. He'd done virtually no work for five months and he hated not writing. In a letter to Perkins he wrote, "My third novel, if I ever write another, will I am sure be black as death with gloom. I should like to sit down with 1/2 dozen chosen companions and drink myself to death but I am sick alike of life, liquor and literature. If it wasn't for Zelda I think I'd disappear out of sight for three years."

The Fitzgeralds' only child, Frances Scott, was born October 26, 1921. She was called Scottie all her life. Despite the comforts and affection of a newborn, that first Minnesota winter was long and tedious for a woman like Zelda who'd grown up in the warm South. She had no friends in St. Paul and the social life was nearly nonexistent.

Fitzgerald worked hard on the proofs of *The Beautiful and Damned.* He fussed excessively over every detail of the jacket design, the advertising, and the publicity. When the book was due to be launched in March, the couple made a whirlwind trip back to New York City—a trip that was, for the most part, a disaster. While the book was successfully launched, both Fitzgeralds were drunk a good deal of the time.

The sales of the book were good, numbering above 40,000. The numbers weren't good enough though, for Fitzgerald was $5,600 in debt to Scribner's at the time. Once again the sting of debt was removed when another deal came through—*This Side of Paradise* was purchased by a movie studio for $10,000.

That summer they moved out to the Yacht Club at White Bear Lake, outside St. Paul. This relieved Zelda of housekeeping duties and kept them near the summer parties. They hired a nurse to care for Scottie while Scott rented a room in town and kept working in high gear.

He started work on a play that was first called *Gabriel's Trombone* and later *The Vegetable.* He had great hopes for this venture and told Max Perkins that it was a great American comedy and the best thing he'd ever written. "After my play is produced," he wrote, "I'll be rich forever and never have to bother you again."

An idea for a new exciting novel was formulating in Fitzgerald's mind during this summer of 1922, but he was somewhat frightened by the fact that he would never have enough money to sustain him to finish it. No matter how much he earned, he was constantly in debt.

Zelda determined she never wanted to spend another winter in Minnesota, so in the fall they made plans to return to New York. For a time they lived at the Plaza while looking for a quiet place in the country. The pressures on them were decidedly less than they'd been two years earlier. Their attempt at living a normal life seemed to be working.

MISSING THE MARK ON BROADWAY

The Fitzgeralds found their country home in Great Neck, Long Island, where they once again sought some type of stability in their lives. They chose a modest home to rent, but they were surrounded by opulence and extravagance. Only 30 minutes from the city, the area of Great Neck was home to many of the well-known Broadway luminaries such as Lillian Russell and George M. Cohan, who held extravagant parties in their palatial mansions. Zelda and Scott were again in their element.

Before long they'd hired a nurse, hired people to run the household, and purchased a secondhand Rolls-Royce. They were ready to begin the wild pace they'd known previously in New York, attending parties among the wealthy and famous of Great Neck, giving a few parties of their own, and finding a few more in the city at the Palais Royal, the Rendezvous, or the Club Gallant. The mornings after, their Japanese houseman often found them asleep on the lawn.

Yet darkness was always on the fringe of the bacchanal. "We were back and we began doing the same things over again and not liking them so much," Fitzgerald wrote. "By this time we knew everybody.... But we were no longer important." At one point, he remarked that "parties are a form of suicide." For both him and Zelda, suicide was never totally out of the question. Scott had first set his date for ending it all at age 30. Later he would move it to age 50, but his early death at age 44 prevented him from doing so.

Among the elite with whom Fitzgerald came in contact was fellow writer Ring Lardner. Lardner, a neighbor of the Fitzgeralds, became Scott's close companion during the year and a half that they lived in Great Neck.

Born Ringgold Wilmer Lardner, in Niles, Michigan, Lardner was 11 years Fitzgerald's senior. By the time the two men met, Lardner had already established his reputation as an acclaimed sports journalist and columnist for various Chicago newspapers. One of Larner's more recognizable traits in his columns, and later in his fiction, was his use of American slang. What some writers had used as a comic effect, Lardner used to produce an authentic American voice. In spite of his humorous side, Larner was a profound cynic, which may have been what drew Fitzgerald to him. Also like Fitzgerald, Lardner had a self-destructive side.

While the two men both hailed from the Midwest, Lardner's intellectual background was not as sophisticated as Fitzgerald's years at

Princeton. However, Fitzgerald had the utmost respect for Lardner's talent and accomplishments and was ever grateful for the kindnesses this veteran writer extended to him. Ring Lardner no doubt provided Fitzgerald more opportunity to delve into deep, at-length talks about writing than any other person until he met Ernest Hemingway.

Fitzgerald convinced Lardner to release a collection of his short stories. The result was the book *How to Write Short Stories (With Samples)*, published in 1924, which met with popular success.

In between parties, Fitzgerald also wrote short stories, which he did to keep money rolling in between his larger works. It was not something he enjoyed. The desperation driving this writing, he believed, killed the freshness and immediacy.

Since his next novel would take a great deal of time, Fitzgerald began to pin more of his hopes on the play, *The Vegetable*. Its success would get him out of debt and finance his next project. Renowned critic Edmund Wilson, one of Fitzgerald's friends from Princeton with whom he kept up continual correspondence, had praised the play, but for a time no Broadway producer was as enthusiastic. When at last a producer was found,Fitzgerald's hopes soared once again.

The play, with the subtitle *From President to Postman*, was a satire about a store clerk named Jerry Frost who becomes president overnight. After this brief period of being president, he reverts back to normal life, this time as a postman, which brings him great happiness. The point was that any man on the street could fill the Oval Office, but that no person in his right mind would want to do so.

As the play was cast and rehearsals were underway, Fitzgerald traveled into New York every day to keep a close eye on the production. The more he saw, the more convinced he was that he had a smash hit on his hands.

However, his elation about the work was dampened by his financial woes. Just before it opened in Atlantic City on November 20, 1923, Fitzgerald desperately wrote to Perkins:

> I have got myself into a terrible mess. As you know for the past month I have been coming every day to the city to rehearsals and then at night writing and making changes on the last act and even on the first two. ... I'm at the end of my rope. ... I owe the Scribner Company something over $3,500.00 ... If I don't in some way get $650 in the bank by Wednesday morning I'll have to pawn the furniture.

The Vegetable may have been written as a political satire, but the audience did not laugh. The characters were too weak to fully engage the audience. Rather than coming alive on the stage, they were merely vehicles for the satire, which was also weak. During the second and third acts on the opening night, the audience began walking out. Fitzgerald, who'd gone to the theater with many of his friends, spent the final act in a bar drowning his disappointment. The show never reached Broadway and never fulfilled Fitzgerald's dreams for financial security. On the contrary, he was deeper in debt than ever before.

Remarkably able to mobilize in an emergency, Fitzgerald stopped drinking, withdrew into a private place (this time to an empty room over his garage) and again wrote with a frenzy. Working 12-hour days for five full weeks, he turned out a volume of short stories that resulted in a steady cash flow. During the winter of 1923-24, Fitzgerald literally worked himself out of debt.

The couple began to look to Europe as a place where they might live more cheaply, and leave the worst of their past behind them. Ever restless, Zelda was never hard to convince about moving. She hated staying in one place for very long. She once commented that she didn't like a room that didn't have a suitcase in it.

By this time, Fitzgerald was finally realizing that he was at least partly to blame for the problems that existed in his life. He revealed this in a letter to Perkins in April 1924:

> It is only in the last four months that I've realized how much I've—well, almost deteriorated in the three years since I finished *The Beautiful and Damned....* If I'd spent this time reading or travelling or doing anything—even staying healthy—it'd be different but I spent it uselessly, neither in study nor in contemplation but only in drinking and raising hell generally.

The time in Great Neck had not, however, been a total loss, for it was here that Fitzgerald found the setting for what would become his most memorable novel, *The Great Gatsby*. When the Fitzgeralds left for Europe in May 1924, Scott may have been weighed down with the overall sense of failure, but he was also buoyed with the hope of writing his best novel.

REVELING ON THE RIVIERA

In the early 1920s, Americans headed to France in droves—to Paris in particular as it evolved into the artistic capital of the world. Here artists, writers, and musicians gathered to meet, to talk, and to work. The city was vibrant and alive with an almost electrifying aura resulting from this vast array of creative energies. The open-air street cafes were among the favorite meeting places for expatriate writers of all varieties.

The Fitzgeralds spent only a short time in Paris before moving in a southerly direction to follow the sunshine. Scott needed a quiet place in which to write. They discovered the perfect place in a villa outside of St. Raphael that looked out over the beaches of the Mediterranean.

Before leaving Paris, however, Scott and Zelda met a wealthy American couple, Gerald and Sara Murphy. The Murphys were the type of people that Fitzgerald dreamed of emulating. Not only were they moneyed, but they were also attractive, witty, and charming. The couple was versed in those areas that marked sophistication—the best wines, the best music, the classics of literature, and both new and old fine art. Unlike many of the Fitzgerald's eccentric friends and acquaintances, the Murphys were a close-knit family with three small children.

Gerald was heir to the Mark Cross luxury leather-goods fortune, and Sara was the daughter of a fabulously wealthy industrialist, Frank Bestow Wiborg. The two had fled to Paris to get away from controlling relatives who didn't approve of their marriage.

Furthermore, the Murphys knew all the right people in Paris, and included the Fitzgeralds in their social events and introduced them around. Gerald was acquainted with the likes of Picasso and Stravinsky, and was considered somewhat of a gifted artist himself.

The Murphys saw in Scott and Zelda the freshness of youth as well as the genius of Scott's literary abilities. They enjoyed one another's company. It was the Murphys who told Scott and Zelda about the south of France, which was then a lovely and unspoiled vacation spot, recently discovered by the Murphys. The two couples agreed to meet there later in the summer, since the Murphys were building a house in the coastal town of Antibes. They never traveled to the Riviera without a large entourage of writers and celebrities.

On June 18, 1924, Fitzgerald wrote to Perkins to report on their situation and to give an update on the novel. "We are idyllicly settled here & the novel is going fine—it ought to be done in a month …"

Fitzgerald had actually started the novel while still in Great Neck and was working on it during the rehearsals for *The Vegetable*. Writing and revising the drama taught Fitzgerald a great deal about writing with more control. The special demands of a play—short scenes and limited time and settings—proved to be an excellent exercise for him. Both of his earlier novels, *This Side of Paradise* and *The Beautiful and Damned*, were loosely structured, and the latter especially dragged on and on with little sense of direction. His newest novel, he declared in an April 1924, letter to Perkins, would be different:

So in my new novel I'm thrown directly on purely creative work—not trashy imaginings as in my stories but the sustained imagination of a sincere and yet radiant world. So I tread slowly and carefully & at times in considerable distress. This book will be a consciously artistic achievement & must depend on that as the 1st books did not.

The lovely landscape and mild climate of the French Riviera allowed Fitzgerald to concentrate fully on the novel. The title of the book, changed by Fitzgerald a number of times, included the following: *Among the Ash-Heaps and Millionaires, On the Road to West Egg, Gold-hatted Gatsby* and *The High-bouncing Lover.* Perkins had preferred *The Great Gatsby.*

Prior to Fitzgerald's leaving New York, Perkins showed him a dust-jacket design drawn by Francis Cugat, depicting the wide brooding eyes of Daisy (a main character from the book) overlooking the carnival-like lights of New York City. From one eye a luminescent green tear is falling. Ernest Hemingway would later say it was the ugliest book cover he'd ever seen, but the Art Deco style appealed to Fitzgerald. In fact, he wrote the eyes into the book as the dominant symbol—the billboard eyes of Dr. T. J. Eckleburg—then informed Perkins in a letter not to give that "jacket" to anyone else!

While Scott worked nonstop on his book, Zelda had to keep herself occupied. However, the French Riviera was virtually unknown at that time, making it a lonely place. While a nurse kept Scottie, Zelda found she had little to do other than retreat to the quiet confines of the beach.

As it happened, there were a number of French aviators who frequented the beach, and one named Edouard Jozan was especially taken with Zelda's beauty and her outgoing personality. Jozan proved to be Fitzgerald's rival. Jozan was daring, brash, and incredibly athletic, while Fitzgerald was intellectual, introspective, and moody. Zelda fell for Jozan and his constant attention.

For a time Fitzgerald was too absorbed in his novel to notice there was even a hint of trouble. However, when he found out the truth, he was devastated. While he might write about infidelity in his novels, such things had no place in his real life.

Fitzgerald handled the matter in a violent and undignified manner. As a result, Jozan departed and Zelda quietly submitted to her husband as she would have done to her father when she was a child. Inwardly, however, she was crushed. A few months later, she would make a suicide attempt with a bottle of sleeping pills. The cracks that had already been forming in their relationship were deepening.

Fitzgerald was deeply sentimental, and he took love very seriously. He had built his entire life around Zelda, and now it seemed that she had let him down. In his notebooks years later he wrote, "That September 1924, I knew something had happened that could never be repaired."

In spite of everything, the façade of the good life had to be maintained, and in October he wrote to his college friend Edmund Wilson, "My book is wonderful, so is the air and the sea. I have got my health back. . . ."

Toward the end of that month, *The Great Gatsby* was finished and sent off to Scribner's. Perkins's reaction was both pleasure and astonishment. He felt it was an incredible work of art. "You once told me," Perkins wrote to Fitzgerald, "you were not a *natural* writer—my God! You have plainly mastered the craft, of course; but you needed far more than craftsmanship for this."

As an editor, Perkins expertly pointed out the rough spots and, as always, Fitzgerald respected his opinions and worked closely with him.

As soon as the book was finished, the Fitzgeralds left the Riviera for Italy, which they liked no more than they did the first time they were there. The weather was disagreeably cold, Scott was again drinking heavily (after having been sober while writing the novel), and the two quarreled bitterly.

During one of his binges, Fitzgerald got in a fight with a taxi driver. In the resulting melee, he hit another man and wound up in jail. While in jail, he was badly beaten, a trauma that would haunt him in the years to come.

In the midst of his hard drinking and marital problems, Fitzgerald worked hard on revisions to the novel. He was meticulous and amazingly objective in editing and polishing his own work, and he would edit up until the last sets of galley proofs, which was a typesetter's nightmare. But since Fitzgerald was such a respected author by this time, no one at Scribner's complained.

Once the revised galleys were submitted in February 1925, Fitzgerald was satisfied to leave any minor copy editing to the proofreaders. He never insisted on seeing page proofs as some other authors did. In fact, his spelling was atrocious and he knew it.

From Rome the Fitzgeralds traveled to Capri for a few weeks, and both of them fell ill, perhaps due to exhaustion from the turmoil. It was here in Capri that Zelda first decided to take up painting, a much needed outlet for her creativity.

The Fitzgeralds left Italy to travel to Paris for the release of *The Great Gatsby*. There would be a greater chance of getting news in Paris than in Rome. During the trip, Fitzgerald wrote to John Peale Bishop, revealing his optimism:

> The cheerfulest things in my life are first Zelda and second the hope that my book has something extraordinary about it. I want

to be extravagantly admired again. Zelda and I sometimes indulge in terrible four-day rows that always start with a drinking party but we're still enormously in love and about the only truly happily married people I know.

The public did not take to *Gatsby* in the way Fitzgerald had hoped. In Marseille on the way to Paris he received a cablegram from Perkins saying the sales looked "doubtful." Fitzgerald hoped the sales would soar up around 75,000, but they barely hit 20,000.

If the sales were disappointing, the reviews were worse. Two days after publication, the *New York World* review stated, "F. Scott Fitzgerald's Latest a Dud." The reviewer for the *Brooklyn Eagle* stated "the boy" was just "puttering around." For what he felt was the very best work of his life, this cool reception cut deeply.

Still, a few people saw the book's true worth. H. L. Mencken tempered his criticism by recognizing the hard work Fitzgerald had poured into the novel. "It shows on every page the results of that laborious effort.... There are pages so artfully contrived that one can no more imagine improvising them than one can imagine improvising a fugue."

The work was acclaimed by a critic named Gilbert Seldes who wrote, "*The Great Gatsby* is a brilliant work, and it is also a sound one; it is carefully written, and vivid; it has structure, and it has life. To all the talents, discipline has been added."

Thankfully, writer friends such as T. S. Eliot and Gertrude Stein wrote him letters of extravagant praise. Max Perkins also continued to believe the book was destined to be a classic. But he also admitted that Fitzgerald might never see the recognition in his lifetime: "One thing I think we can be sure of: that when the tumult and shouting of the rabble of reviewers and gossipers dies, The Great Gatsby will stand out as a very extraordinary book."

As usual, Maxwell Perkins's perception was absolutely correct.

BEGINNING TO CRACK

The Fitzgeralds lived in Paris the following summer in a rented apartment located in the center of the city at 14 rue de Tilsitt. It was a difficult time for Scott. He later would call it the summer of "1,000 parties and no work."

The so-called failure of *Gatsby* confused and embittered Fitzgerald. He desperately tried to figure out what was wrong with the book, blaming first the title and then the fact that the female characters weren't strong enough.

Of course, the blame lay with neither one. He felt he was at a crucial juncture in his life. If he could not make a living writing novels, what else was left? He came to despise short-story writing. He could whip them out quickly and they brought in good income, but he felt they were not his best work. Above all else, he loved writing novels.

When Scott and Zelda first arrived in Paris in the spring of 1924, Scott had become acquainted with a young writer named Ernest Hemingway. He was an unknown outside the expatriate group in Paris. Fitzgerald took an immediate liking to Hemingway, admiring his writing skills as well as his brusque no-nonsense personality. As soon as the Fitzgeralds returned to Paris from the Riviera in 1925, Scott contacted Hemingway and the two met at the Dingo Bar. Even though Fitzgerald drank himself into a stupor through the course of the evening, the two became good friends.

Fitzgerald was able to reach out and help this young writer at a time when his own career was at the breaking point. His interest in Hemingway's work led to Scribner's publishing a collection of Hemingway's short stories. Later, Fitzgerald would lend valuable editing advice on Hemingway's novel, *The Sun Also Rises*. The two men went on to have a rocky but enduring friendship through the years.

Zelda and Hemingway, however, disliked one another from the outset. Hemingway saw Zelda as a meddler who was jealous of her husband's work. He felt she was the cause for Scott's drinking problem and stated that Scott might have remained sober if Zelda had not dragged him off to every drunken party. Zelda, in turn, thought Hemingway was a big fake.

In the meantime, Scott and Zelda's marriage was deteriorating quickly. Scott's alcoholism was in full bloom, and Zelda's behavior was becoming increasingly erratic. At a dinner party in August, attended by the famed dancer Isadora Duncan, Scott angered Zelda by going over to Duncan's table to talk. In a disturbing display of self-destruction, Zelda purposely flung herself down a flight of stairs. The guests sat stunned for a moment, wondering if she had killed herself. She was in fact not seriously hurt—at least not physically.

At the end of August, Scott and Zelda traveled to the Murphys' home in Antibes for a month. There they hobnobbed with screen stars, writers, wealthy heirs and heiresses, and political leaders—some of the best-known celebrities of the day. While Scott and Zelda greatly admired the Murphys and coveted their lifestyle, they were unable to grasp that the Murphy's friendships with these people had developed over years. Scott and Zelda were like two children who could not bear it if they were not the center of attention wherever they went.

At Antibes, Fitzgerald started working on his fourth novel, which would eventually become *Tender is the Night*. He used the Murphys' home, Villa

America, as the setting, and the hero of the story, Dick Diver, is based on Gerald Murphy. The opening scene of the book takes place on the beach adjacent to the Murphys' villa.

Progress on the book was extremely slow, however. There were too many distracting parties in Paris that winter. By this time, Fitzgerald was hopelessly addicted to alcohol. While the city of Paris was alive and exciting, the Fitzgeralds were too intoxicated to see it. While they were once the stars of any party, they were now considered vulgar. And whereas once Fitzgerald could intersperse hard work with his drinking, that was no longer the case. The Murphys alone remained consistently supportive of both Scott and Zelda and seemed genuinely concerned about their welfare. Perkins received a letter from Fitzgerald saying, "You remember I used to say that I wanted to die at thirty—well I'm twenty-nine and the prospect is still welcome."

Thankfully, the new year of 1926 brought a few brighter moments for Fitzgerald. In January, Max wrote to him that Owen Davis had adapted *The Great Gatsby* for a stage presentation. Following its success on Broadway, it was purchased by a Hollywood movie producer. Perkins assured Fitzgerald that the story line had been maintained better than either of them could have hoped.

Although he continued to dislike short story writing, Fitzgerald's stories were now selling to *The Saturday Evening Post* for more than $2,000 each. A collection of his short stories entitled *All the Sad Young Men* was published and received rave reviews. *All the Sad Young Men* sold well, giving the Fitzgeralds a momentary reprieve from the weight of extreme debt. A letter to Max in March mentions that Fitzgerald was out of debt for the first time in four years.

While positive things were taking place Stateside, Scott had taken Zelda to a remote place in the Pyrenees to take a cure for her alcoholism. In bits and pieces he continued work on his novel, but it was painfully slow. By summer they were considering a return to the States. Max encouraged Fitzgerald to come home and live in a "typical community," and suggested Wilmington, Delaware.

At the close of 1926, they did return to America with plans to find that quiet place and settle down where Fitzgerald could get a lot of work done. The prince and princess of the Jazz Age returned home ragged and weary, both full-blown alcoholics.

No sooner had they arrived home than an offer from Hollywood infused Scott with new hope. The plans for quiet living would have to wait— United Artists studio wanted Fitzgerald to write a movie script for their star, Constance Talmadge. Fitzgerald had considered abandoning novel writing and casting his lot in the movie capital. Now was his chance.

Hollywood was a fresh and upcoming town in the 1920s. Movie stars were becoming nationally known celebrities, and the town fairly glittered with money and opportunities. Scott and Zelda were whisked right into the swing of things as they lunched at Pickfair (the home of Mary Pickford and Douglas Fairbanks), and attended parties with stars such as Lillian Gish, Lois Moran, John Barrymore, and Richard Barthelmess. The fresh young star, Lois Moran, fascinated Fitzgerald; later he would put his feelings about her into the character of Rosemary Hoyt in *Tender Is the Night.*

Living in their fashionable apartment at the Ambassador Hotel, the Fitzgeralds were treated as though they too were stars. Being the center of attention once again assuaged their insecurities. However, at the many parties they attended, they ended up playing frantic jokes and pranks that few guests thought amusing.

When Fitzgerald finally completed the script for the movie *Lipstick*, it was rejected. The Fitzgeralds reacted badly. They piled the hotel furniture in the middle of the room, put their unpaid bills on top, and left the movie capital.

They decided to take Max's advice and located an enormous, stately mansion called Ellerslie, near Wilmington, Delaware. Here Fitzgerald hoped to find the peace and quiet he needed to finish the novel. In January 1928, Fitzgerald wrote to Max that he'd been sober since October. However, the lack of social stimulation agitated the couple and they quarreled continuously. Moments alone together were what Fitzgerald called an "organized cat and dog fight." The bright spot and unifying force in their lives was Scottie, who was turning out to be a delightful child.

As before, while Scott threw himself into his novel, Zelda was restless and bored. She harbored a deep desire to write and had published a few articles, but this interest wilted under her husband's shadow. She turned to painting, but still was not satisfied. Finally, she took up dancing, which she had loved as a child.

At 28, she was too old and unhealthy for such rigor, and had inadvertently set herself up for failure. No one attempted to talk her out of the idea, but then no one could foresee that she would pursue success with such a dangerous compulsive intensity. Several times a week, Zelda traveled to Philadelphia to pursue her dream of becoming a professional ballet dancer. It was at this time she first began to suffer from the uncomfortable skin condition, eczema.

In April 1928, with the excuse that Zelda wanted to further her studies in ballet, the Fitzgeralds once again packed their belongings and sailed for Paris. They rented an apartment at 58 rue de Vaugirard, and faced another long, unproductive, unhappy summer, during which their quarrels grew more intense than ever. Scott openly resented the discipline and concentration Zelda poured into her dancing, spurred by his difficulty in concentrating on his novel.

At this time, Fitzgerald became acquainted with two women, Sylvia Beach and Adrienne Monnier, owners and operators of the expatriates' bookstore, Shakespeare and Company. They admired Fitzgerald and were enamored with his recklessness. That summer he also met the Irish writer James Joyce, whom Fitzgerald greatly admired. These new friends gave a momentary brightness to an otherwise bleak time, for most of their old friends now avoided them.

In September, the Fitzgerald's returned to Ellerslie where Scott's drinking became unpredictable and volatile. "Thirty two years old," he wrote in his ledger for 1928, "and sore ... about it." Another entry was underscored: "OMINOUS. No Real Progress in ANY way & wrecked myself with dozens of people." Entries during that preceding summer read, "June—Carried home from the Ritz; July—Drinking and general unpleasantness—first trip to jail; August—second trip jail—general carelessness and boredom."

While he wrote letters to Perkins saying the novel was coming along well, it was in fact not coming along at all. He even went so far as to promise two chapters a month, but had no power to keep that promise. In the spring of 1929, the Fitzgaralds once again chose to return to Paris.

As the marriage continued to disintegrate, Zelda grew more remote from both Scott and Scottie. Her behavior became impetuous and unpredictable. When summer came, they returned to the Riviera, but everything had changed. Tourists had invaded the once-quiet beaches and few people remembered, or were interested in, the Fitzgeralds. Scott resorted to more immature attention-seeking measures, such as throwing fruit at guests and hurling wineglasses over a garden wall. The Murphys, ever patient, finally banished the Fitzgeralds from their home for three weeks.

They returned to Paris for the winter, which was cold and miserable. Other than a brief trip to Algiers in February, they remained in Paris until spring. Zelda did get one or two small engagements as a ballet dancer, but the big role she constantly dreamed of never materialized. She simply worked harder and harder and grew more and more tense.

In April, Zelda was at a luncheon with friends when they noticed she was becoming agitated. After announcing she was late for her ballet class, one of the friends offered to accompany her. In the taxi, Zelda grew so upset she began to shake. When the cab slowed to a standstill because of a snarl in traffic, she jumped out and began to run to the studio. This incident gave one of the more concrete signs that Zelda was seriously ill.

On April 30, she entered a hospital outside Paris and remained there for nine days. On May 22, after hearing voices and experiencing delusions, she entered a clinic in Switzerland. The stay was again short. On June 5, she entered Les Rives de Pragins at Nyon, near Geneva. Here she received the diagnosis of schizophrenia. Scott was told that she had one chance in four of total recovery, and two chances in four of a partial recovery.

For several months, she refused to see Scott. In fact, the doctors informed him that one of the things that tormented her in her delirium was his drinking. When she did see him, she suffered from severe attacks of eczema. Scott felt great sympathy and concern for Zelda—in addition to the guilt of knowing he was partly to blame for her breakdown. He lived in Swiss hotels to remain close even when he was not allowed to see her. Scottie was at school in Paris.

During her stay at Pragins, Zelda wrote stories that she eventually showed to Scott. He liked them and attempted to get Perkins to see about publishing them, but Perkins gently and wisely refused.

Much of what happened during this time, in one way or another, found its way into Scott's future writings. While he still had little control over his drinking, he was able to remain sober long enough to turn out a few stories to remain gainfully employed. By this time, his price for short stories had climbed up to $4,000. During the 15 months that Zelda was in the hospital in Switzerland, he wrote 12 short stories.

In January 1931, Scott received word that his father, Edward Fitzgerald, had died. Scott returned to America to attend the funeral. This return also provided him with the opportunity to travel to Montgomery and tell Zelda's family about her illness.

Upon his return to Switzerland, he found Zelda sufficiently recovered to leave the hospital and travel. They took a trip to Lake Annecy, France, where they attempted to recapture some of the old romance. Scott would later refer to it as one of the happiest times of their lives.

In September 1931, they returned to America and settled in Montgomery, where Zelda could be near her family and Scott could quietly finish his novel.

FURTHER DECLINE

Back in Montgomery, Zelda's family and friends could hardly mask their shock at seeing her changed appearance. The once vibrant and beautiful Zelda now looked haggard, her eyes sunken and the freshness gone. Scott and Zelda had barely settled into a rented house on Felder Avenue in Montgomery when he received word from his agent that Hollywood had promised another deal. Metro-Goldwyn-Mayer offered to pay Scott $1,200 a week to write a script based on a novel titled *Red-Headed Woman*. He was in no position to refuse, since he was, as usual, deeply in debt.

Leaving Zelda and Scottie in Montgomery, he returned to Hollywood. As had happened to Zelda in Montgomery, old friends in Hollywood barely recognized the once-confident Fitzgerald. Now he was nervous and withdrawn, and could only find solace in alcohol.

The script was a failure. Seven years later he would sum up this experience in a letter to Scottie:

> I was jittery underneath and beginning to drink more than I ought to. Far from approaching it too confidently I was far too humble. I ran afoul of a bastard named de Sano, since a suicide, and let myself be gypped out of command. I wrote the picture and he changed as I wrote.... Result—a bad script. I left with the money, for this was a contract for weekly payments, but disillusioned and disgusted, vowing never to go back, tho they said it wasn't my fault and asked me to stay.

While Scott was away, Judge Sayre died in November, throwing Zelda into a dangerous asthma attack. She grew hysterical over the loss of her father, which spelled the end of any type of security or stability in her life. In January she suffered another total breakdown.

Fitzgerald hurried home to find that his wife would have to be hospitalized once again. On February 12, 1932, Zelda was admitted to the Henry Phipps Psychiatric Clinic of Johns Hopkins University outside of Baltimore. Scott took a suite at the Hotel Rennert in Baltimore to be near her.

Prior to Judge Sayre's death, Zelda had begun writing a novel of her own—*Save Me the Waltz*. While at Phipps, she finished the largely autobiographical work and sent it straight to Max Perkins without her husband's knowledge. When Scott found out, he reacted as though his worst rival had just stolen his best idea. He wasn't far from wrong since she used verbatim much of the material from Scott's new novel.

The rivalry between the two, which had simmered for many years, finally boiled to the surface. Zelda's defiance cut deeply. What Scott perceived to be a direct betrayal bothered him long afterward. Both *Save Me the Waltz* and *Tender Is the Night* are depressing books because both follow so closely the tragic lives of Scott and Zelda.

Later, when his anger subsided, Fitzgerald worked with Perkins to see to it that Zelda's work was published. By then he realized that she needed the sense of success that a published book would bring to her. The book required a good deal of editing to tone down the outward attacks on Scott. Eventually, he could report to Perkins that the novel "is good now, improved in every way." However, when it came out in the fall of 1932, it received nothing but negative reviews and sold poorly.

When Scott saw that Zelda's condition was not improving he decided to move himself and Scottie to a large, rambling Victorian house on the Bayard Turnbull estate at Rodgers Forge, next door to the Phipps Clinic.

During the summer of 1932, Zelda was able to join her husband and daughter at La Paix, and the strain on Scott was enormous. In addition to caring for an unstable wife and a young daughter, his income had dropped to barely half of what it had been in previous years. The whole country reeled from the onslaught of the Great Depression, and the economy had bottomed out. Books and magazines were not priorities when people didn't have enough money for a loaf of bread. At the same time, Fitzgerald had lost the ability to turn out a quick short story. The vicious cycle took its toll—he needed to drink in order to write, and yet he was unable to write due to his drunkenness. As his physical health continued to fail, the psychiatrists with whom he spoke in regard to Zelda's case warned him that he too was in danger of an emotional breakdown.

Throughout the summer at La Paix, Zelda painted and wrote fiction. Scott felt obliged to assist her in her writing projects. However, beneath the surface he resented her writing. He was the writer in the family, and it was his writing that kept the food on the table and the rent paid.

When Zelda's erratic behavior grew particularly violent and excessive, Scott investigated the possibility of getting a divorce, since it was obvious the two were destroying one another. He never went through with it, his sense of obligation was too great.

He continued devoting long hours to the novel, working late into the night and often wandering the halls of the large house in his threadbare bathrobe as he thought out the scenes. When Zelda inadvertently started a fire by burning old clothes in a faulty fireplace, the house was afterward in need of repair. Fitzgerald begged the landlord to wait to have the work done until after his novel was finished. He could abide with no interruptions or distractions.

In September 1933, Fitzgerald's dear friend Ring Lardner died. In his grief Fitzgerald wrote a piece about the acclaimed writer for *The New Republic* magazine.

Before the end of the year, the family had moved to a smaller house at 1307 Park Avenue in Baltimore, to cut down on expenses. In the ensuing months, Fitzgerald pressed on to complete the novel while negotiating for the magazine serializations. It was eventually taken by *Scribner's Magazine* and published January to April 1934. He was mostly living on advances from Scribner's for the upcoming book.

After the novel was finished, he pushed himself into a frenzied period of turning out five short stories for the *Post*. Zelda, during this same period, suffered yet another breakdown and entered Sheppard-Pratt Hospital in January. With each subsequent breakdown, any hope of her full recovery was lessened. (Zelda would, for the most part, spend the remainder of her life in an institution.)

In March, the doctors at Sheppard-Pratt suggested she be transferred to Craig House in upstate New York for better care. She stayed there for nine weeks, during which time Scott remained in Baltimore, as spousal visits were discouraged. Fitzgerald wrote a series of letters to Dr. Jonathan Slocum at Craig House asking dozens of unanswerable questions regarding Zelda's prognosis. While she received excellent care at this facility, her illness by this time was quite severe and seemingly incurable

With this latest news, Fitzgerald now focused his hopes and dreams on his novel. The serialized version brought in limited praise from other writers such as Marjorie Rawlings, author of *The Yearling*, who had long been a fan of Fitzgerald's work. This did not alleviate his extreme nervousness as the release date for *Tender Is the Night* drew near. He tortured himself, wondering whether he was or was not still a gifted writer. He had lived with the characters of this book for so long—seven years—that they had become more authentic to him than real people.

The book was released in April 1934 to a dismal reception. Because of his emotional attachment, Fitzgerald was deeply hurt at the public's cool reception of the novel. So absorbed was he in the book, he seemed unaware that the content—stories of wealthy couples cavorting on the French Riviera—had long gone out of fashion. Popular novels in the 1930s had to do with the rights of the working man, not the frivolities of the wealthy. Fitzgerald's objective view, a few years later, was that if he'd written it cold the quality of the writing would have been higher. As with his previous novels, Fitzgerald labored over the galley proofs, working extensively on the edits. Similar to *Gatsby*, the book presents a vivid historical account of the era of the '20s.

Once the book was out, as was the custom by Scribner's, a volume of Fitzgerald's short stories was released entitled *Taps at Reveille*. He struggled in an almost mechanical fashion editing the stories and readying them for submission. This book also met with bad reviews. He had to face a number of cold frightening facts: his marriage had failed, his sick wife was beyond his help, his debt load would not be lessened since the books were unsuccessful, his health was deteriorating (cirrhosis of the liver and tuberculosis), and his battle to stay sober seemed hopelessly lost. He never considered the options of putting Scottie in public schools and Zelda in a public institution.

Under the weight of these circumstances, Fitzgerald fled—not so much to escape, as to face who he was and to find himself. He wound up in Hendersonville, near Asheville, North Carolina, where he lived frugally and attempted to put himself on the wagon again. For the next few months he would bounce about from Hendersonville to Asheville to Baltimore and back to Asheville once again.

Ironically, while living in an apartment in the Cambridge Arms opposite the Johns Hopkins campus, he could see from his window the monument to Francis Scott Key, the famous ancestor for whom he'd been named.

At this low ebb, Fitzgerald wrote out his thoughts and feelings, resulting in three articles, eventually to be published in *Esquire* magazine, entitled "The Crack-Up." In these articles, he openly and without shame described his meteoric rise to fame and his subsequent plummet into failure. He referred to himself as a cracked plate, but goes on to say that even a cracked plate can be kept to hold crackers late at night or leftovers in the ice box. Certainly he had cause to wonder if he was at all worth saving.

The essays, published the first three months of 1936, brought attention to him again even though they emphasized his failures. Even though they are autobiographical, they have the intense feel of good fiction. His friend Ernest Hemingway was greatly offended by the tone of surrender in the essays, and said as much to Scott in a letter.

In the spring of 1936, Scott finally settled in Asheville and in April, Zelda entered Asheville's Highland Hospital. There she would spend the greater portion of the remainder of her life.

In July, as his health was somewhat improved, Fitzgerald attempted to show off his athletic skills by executing a difficult dive from a 15-foot board. The result was badly torn shoulder muscles, and his shoulder was eventually encased in a heavy plaster cast. Friends in Asheville helped to rig up a writing board so he could continue to work, albeit only for brief periods of time.

Just as he was learning to get around balancing the heavy weight of the cast, he fell in his bathroom and was forced to lie on the floor for a time, causing a mild form of arthritis. This put him into bed for an extra five weeks. Being bedridden halted his work and in his depression he went back to drinking. His income for the year had amounted to about $10,000, and his debts amounted to four times that amount. His luck, however, was about to turn one more time.

While he was recuperating, Fitzgerald received word that his mother had died. He wanted to attend her funeral, but travel was out of the question. Her death affected him more than he thought it would, since they had never been close. He resented her more than he loved her, and through the years he corresponded with her only occasionally. However, her death brought him into an inheritance of close to $20,000 at a point when he desperately needed it. With this, he would pay off some of his debts and have at least a temporary relief.

Scottie, now a pretty and personable teenager, attended the elite Ethel Walker's prep school in Connecticut. She somehow had received a remission of tuition. As her father before her, she was the poor among the rich; however, the situation didn't seem to have the same effect on her as it did on her father.

While Fitzgerald loved his daughter deeply, he was relentless in his correction of her behavior and overly strict in his demands with regard to her activities. In his letters to her he demanded the very discipline in her studies that he so painfully lacked when he attended school. In spite of his limited resources he sent her cash when she needed it and arranged a dance party for her at the Hotel Belvedere in Baltimore at Christmas break, 1936.

While the inheritance money gave him a limited reprieve, it was clear Fitzgerald would have to have some sort of substantial income for the future care of his wife and daughter. He let his agent, Harold Ober, know that he was willing to give Hollywood one last chance. This time, he was prepared to take the town by storm and perhaps become a noted director.

THE FAIRYTALE ENDS

Fitzgerald's return to Hollywood was fueled by fantasy, not just of riches but of artistic success. He felt he could avoid the usual mistakes this time and rise to the pinnacle of the movie profession. On the train west, he wrote these thoughts in a letter to Scottie:

> I must be very tactful but keep my hand on the wheel from the start—find out the key man among the bosses and the most malleable among the collaborators—then fight the rest tooth and nail until, in fact or in effect, I'm alone on the picture. That's the only way I can do my best work. Given a break I can make them double this contract in less [than] two years.

As brash as this sounds, it was modest in comparison to what he actually desired. What he really wanted was a position similar to that of Irving Thalberg, the director who had absolute power over all his pictures. (Fitzgerald's character Monroe Stahr in his novel *The Last Tycoon* would be based on the life of Thalberg.) The heady thoughts seemed to infuse him with new life.

Ironically, his outward appearance belied this inner excitement. Old friends hardly recognized Scott, describing him as thin, pale, frightened, and nervous.

His prearranged salary was set at $1,000 a week, a fortune in the mid-1930s, when so many people were out of work. He arranged to have his salary sent to Ober, his agent, so that a certain amount would be applied to his debts. Ober gave only a small amount to Fitzgerald, who determined he would make do on what was left. Even when he was desperate for money, he maintained this arrangement, which ensured continual care for Zelda and Scottie.

Fitzgerald moved into the Garden of Allah Hotel, where he lived amidst other well-known movie scriptwriters. The first picture he worked on was *A Yank at Oxford*. He threw himself enthusiastically into the work, making every effort to master new skills. While his contribution was not used, still he felt he'd learned a great deal.

The next film was a comedy entitled *Three Comrades*, the results of which pleased him to some degree. It looked as though, for the time being at least, he could handle this kind of work even though his expertise and abilities were not recognized or respected. By and large, F. Scott Fitzgerald was a forgotten man; many people thought he was dead.

In spite of the social whirl that beckoned at every turn, Fitzgerald was able, for once in his life, to turn his back on it. Invitations came, but he was able to remain sober and wrote to friends back east—Perkins included—numbering how many months he'd remained sober. Perhaps it was the miles between him and Zelda that allowed him to look upon the "last year and a half in Baltimore and Carolina as a long nightmare …"

He did happen to attend one party at Robert Benchley's, where he found the answer to some of his current problems. Here he was introduced to the beautiful Sheilah Graham, a famous Hollywood columnist.

Sheilah came from an interesting background. Born Lily Sheil in London's East End, she spent her early years in an orphanage because her mother was unable financially to care for her. At the orphanage, the girls' heads were shaved for sanitation reasons. This sense of shame had a profound effect on Sheilah. She chose to later change her name and embellish her identity and, in essence, live a lie, much like Jay Gatsby. Using her own powers of tremendous will, she became a chorus girl, then acted onstage before becoming a writer. She had arrived in America only a few months before meeting Fitzgerald, and at that time she was engaged to Lord Donegall.

Fitzgerald and Sheilah fell in love almost instantly. Sheilah soon broke off her former engagement, giving up a life of wealth as a Lady in London's high society to cast her lot with F. Scott Fitzgerald, whom she barely knew. Like the windfall from his inheritance, meeting Sheilah was an extraordinary stroke of luck for Scott. He now had someone to love and to care about—someone to live for.

At first, Sheilah knew nothing of Fitzgerald's alcoholism, but when she discovered the truth, she faced it with great courage. It was because of her that he found the strength to remain sober for longer and longer periods of time.

His work, however, was going badly. His script for *Three Comrades*, which he labored over for months, was edited to pieces in one weekend by the film's producer, Joseph Mankiewicz. A wounded Fitzgerald wrote a sad letter to Mankiewicz practically begging him to restore the script, to no avail. This movie contained the only film credit he ever received and yet it wasn't even his own work. Fitzgerald had grown accustomed to working by himself on his own creations—his sensitive writer personality was at a loss as to how to endure such attacks.

The next picture, *Infidelity*, starred Joan Crawford but was killed by the censors who found the film morally suspect. With each successive blow, Fitzgerald's discouragement grew. Subsequent script assignments became nothing more than jobs to him. Still, he was thankful that his contract was renewed at the end of the year and raised to $1,250 a week.

On occasion, Scott returned to North Carolina to take Zelda on outings, mainly out of a sense of duty. They nearly always resulted in disaster.

In November 1938, producer Walter Wanger called on Fitzgerald to do a script about the Dartmouth Winter Carnival. Wanger paired Fitzgerald with a young writer named Budd Schulberg. While Schulberg had long been an admirer of Fitzgerald, he confessed to Wanger that he thought the writer had been dead for years.

It was Wanger's idea for Fitzgerald and Schulberg to actually travel to the Dartmouth campus and research the carnival firsthand. Fitzgerald had been ill and Sheilah was terribly worried about him—so much so that she flew on the same flight, but sat discreetly in another row. On the plane Fitzgerald began to drink and was unable to stop.

Sheilah parted ways with them in New York, where she planned to take care of business while Fitzgerald and Schulberg went on to the college campus. Fitzgerald had been hired as the veteran writer who would add the right literary touches to the film. But he wasn't coherent enough to speak rationally with those he met on campus. He made an ugly spectacle of himself as he wandered around in a daze. One evening after drinking heavily at a fraternity party, he met face-to-face with Wanger, who fired him on the spot. When he once again met up with Sheilah, she insisted he remain in the hospital in New York for a couple of weeks until he was sufficiently recovered to return to California.

The incident at Dartmouth created a series of problems for Fitzgerald. His contract with MGM for 1939 was not renewed. For a time he freelanced but found work only sporadically. Early in 1939, he wrote to Perkins that he was involved with the scriptwriting for *Gone With the Wind*, and lamented that he was not allowed to use any dialogue other than direct quotes from the book. A great number of writers were called in on this script, and, like them, Fitzgerald didn't last long.

He attempted to begin another novel, but was unable to work on it except for short periods of time. Again he faced the fear of not having enough to pay for Zelda's care and Scottie's tuition at Vassar. He once again began drinking heavily, and now Sheilah received the brunt of his rage. During one brawl he threatened to kill her, but she was able to call the police while he was searching for the gun. Terrified, she was ready to leave him, but stayed with him.

In another of his last-ditch efforts, Fitzgerald decided to return east and take Zelda on a trip to Cuba. True to form, a drunken Fitzgerald got into a terrible fight with some locals when he attempted to stop a cockfight. Once again, he found himself in the hospital on his return home.

Once back in Hollywood, Fitzgerald decided to write his own screenplay. But now, he'd gotten in a row with Harold Ober, his agent. Ober had continually loaned Fitzgerald money, and he and his wife had acted as surrogate parents to Scottie, often keeping her in their home. But Fitzgerald grew angry when Ober at last refused to loan out any more advances, and the relationship was severed.

Eventually, Scott and Sheilah reconciled and she encouraged him to return to work on his novel. The novel, entitled *The Last Tycoon*, centered around Hollywood and the personalities that created the glamorous myths of "Tinseltown" during its golden era. In September 1939, *Collier's* magazine expressed interest in Fitzgerald's novel and offered him an enormous sum if he would submit 15,000 words and an outline by a certain date. Fitzgerald jumped at the chance, but by now his health was such that he could barely work a few hours a day. Because he was unable to produce what they needed, he broke with *Collier's* in a typical rage.

When 1940 dawned, bringing with it the promise of a fresh new decade, Fitzgerald's mood was once again on the upswing. For almost the entire year, he remained sober and worked steadily on his novel. In a letter to Zelda on October 23, he wrote: "I am deep in the novel, living in it, and it makes me happy.... Two thousand words today and all good."

On November 2, he wrote: "The novel is hard as pulling teeth but that is because it is in its early character-planting phase.... It means welding together hundreds of stray impressions and incidents to form the fabric of entire personalities. But later it should go faster."

His room was full of charts, showing the different movements of each character. He was certain that this novel would the redemption that he'd wanted for so long.

In early December, a mild heart attack put him into bed, but he continued to write using a special wooden desk. On December 20, Sheilah talked him into attending a movie with her. As they were preparing to leave at the conclusion, Fitzgerald experienced severe chest pains, and Sheilah had to assist him out to the car. Because his doctor was scheduled to visit the next afternoon, they decided not to call him that evening.

The next morning Fitzgerald had slept well and was feeling much better. After lunch he was reading an article about the Princeton football team while waiting for the doctor to arrive. Suddenly, he stood up from his chair, grabbed at the mantel and fell to the floor. He was dead within a few minutes.

EPILOGUE

Fitzgerald had asked to be buried in the Catholic cemetery at Rockville, but the Church would not allow it and he was buried in the Rockville Union Cemetery.

Eight years later in March 1948, a fire swept through the Highland Hospital in Asheville. Zelda was trapped in a room on the top floor and burned to death. She was buried beside her husband and they share a common headstone.

Interest in F. Scott Fitzgerald began to bloom almost a decade following his death. In the 1950s, book after book was reissued, followed by new collections of short stories. Later, a student's edition of *The Great Gatsby* was released and became established in the academic canon. When the Scribner Library was established in 1960 (a series of best-selling classics in paperback), *The Great Gatsby* took its place at the top of the bestseller list and never moved. Eventually Scribner's was publishing no less than seven editions of the book.

Fitzgerald's greatest strength was his storytelling ability. He was able to turn out almost 100 or so short stories in addition to his major novels in the course of his lifetime. He was, years after this death, at last recognized as a serious novelist. In addition, Fitzgerald was an artful writer, paying special attention to the smallest details of description and characterization.

His weakness overall was the waste of his gifts—waste of health and life and energy and talent. By squandering too much too early with no thought of temperance in any area, F. Scott Fitzgerald lived a greater tragedy than any of the characters he created.

THOMAS HEISE

The *"Purposeless Splendor"* of the Ideal in the Fiction of F. Scott Fitzgerald

No major American novelist of the 1920s generation was more enamored with a lifestyle of excess and pleasure than F. Scott Fitzgerald. None of them leveled a more devastating critique of it either. Fitzgerald came to maturity during America's giddy post-World War I economic prosperity—a time perfectly suited to his personality—and held the national spotlight for almost a decade. His celebrity began with the publication of *This Side of Paradise* (1920) when he was only 23 years old, was guaranteed by the notorious *The Beautiful and Damned* two years later, and reached its culmination with *The Great Gatsby* (1925), his most enduring novel of wealth and corruption. Nine years later, when Fitzgerald finally got around to publishing his next book, *Tender Is the Night*, it found a cool reception, was judged seriously flawed, and given its subject—the peregrinations and travails of well-heeled, expatriate Americans—it was considered to be out of touch with the new economic realities of the Depression. As the nation sank, so did Fitzgerald's own life. He wasted much of the '30s drowning in alcoholism and carousing with the rich in Paris, while his beautiful wife, Zelda Sayre, checked in and out of mental institutions for her worsening schizophrenia. Reflecting on the 'lost' years after the success of *The Great Gatsby*, Fitzgerald wrote, "I have been a poor caretaker of everything I possessed, even of my talent". When he died in 1940 of a heart attack at the age of 44, his novels were no longer carried in most bookstores. *The Last Tycoon* was unfinished. Zelda would perish in a fire eight years later. "[T]he party," as Nick Carraway pithily sums up at *The Great Gatsby*'s end, "was over."

It is hard not to draw parallels between Fitzgerald's rise to fame in the 1920s, followed by his collapse in 1930s and the surging American economy of the same time period that would fall meteorically with the stock market plunge on October 29, 1929. The culture's sudden love affair with glamour and advertising, its delight in the mass production of consumer goods, radios tuned to the new beats of jazz, automobiles speeding down the nation's freshly laid highways, the creation of mass-circulation magazines that catered to an appetite for entertainment and leisure and that helped give birth to the 'new' woman and the new icon—the flapper—and the ease with which money was made and spent and made again: these have all become the hallmarks of the 1920s. It was the age of the beauty parlor and new appliances in newer and bigger homes. The number of cars in America tripled in the decade after the war, and the number of women smoking in public shot up even faster. Not everyone shared in the spectacular wealth and optimism, but most of the people in Fitzgerald's novels did. Whether frolicking in the fountain of New York's plush Plaza Hotel, as a young Fitzgerald once boasted to have done, or turning out lyrical prose that momentarily captured the era's atmosphere of "chatter and laughter, and casual innuendo . . . and enthusiastic meetings between women who never knew each other's names," as he would become famous for doing, Fitzgerald's life and work were indebted to the postwar generation's infatuation with an elegance that often spilled over into hedonism. And in return, the carefree, adventurous ethic of the young and beautiful of the '20s found expression through Fitzgerald. It was a spirit that produced its most lasting symbol with jazz. In reference to the syncopated rhythms and sudden improvisations of this innovative music, Fitzgerald affectionately called the decade after the war the Jazz Age. Others would label it the Roaring Twenties so as to conjure up the revving engines of roadsters that, much like Fitzgerald's own novels, helped harness the freedom, independence, and raw energy of the period.

If the '20s is a story that begins with unbridled American optimism, then it is one that ends with a good deal of disillusionment, cynicism, and introspection. It is also a story written by Fitzgerald. The dark silences between notes and the wrecked cars that dotted the nation's roadways in the years before the great crash of 1929 are chronicled in the lives of Amory Blaine, Anthony and Gloria Patch, and most memorably by Jay Gatsby's next door neighbor, Nick Carraway. Fitzgerald's first three novels, written years before "the party was over," partake in the revelry, but they are also prescient, permeated as they are with the sense that it was all about to unravel. The Roaring Twenties was a hit-and-run culture for Fitzgerald, one in which "careless people . . . smashed up things and creatures and then retreated back into their money or their vast carelessness or whatever it was that kept them together" (*Gatsby* 139). After the car accident that kills Myrtle and after the murder of Gatsby at the hands of her husband, Gatsby's mansion stands as a "huge incoherent failure," one that we can be sure will fall like other famous houses in American fiction. The novel's ebullient opening descriptions of Gatsby's life and luxury turn increasingly dark, until the lights in the house are turned off altogether. Likewise, Dick Diver's breakdown in the summer of 1929 in the later novel *Tender Is the Night* is most certainly a harbinger of the more severe collapse during the fall of that same year, when the nation's economy was found to be built on sand. Too heavily financed on credit, the new consumer economy was structurally unsound. Given the inflated stock portfolios, the stagnant wages among the working class, and a persistent agricultural depression, the financial meltdown seems in retrospect inevitable. For a generation that came of age "to find all Gods dead, all wars fought, all faiths in man shaken," the emotional crash found in nearly every Fitzgerald work, and found in many American families as they struggled to get by or to buy more, also seems unavoidable (*This Side* 255).

The late-night parties in Fitzgerald's fiction, metaphors for the era's "purposeless splendor," often dissipate into "haunting loneliness" that speaks to a larger sense of disconnect that Fitzgerald heard murmuring beneath the tempo of the upbeat music (*Gatsby* 47, 62). It is this sense of isolation and sadness and the still-clung-to possibility of companionship that Fitzgerald describes when he recalls how "[p]eople disappeared, reappeared, made plans to go somewhere, and then lost each other, searched for each other, found each other a few feet away" (*Gatsby* 31). As a member of a coterie of American writers living in Paris in the 1920s which included Ernest Hemingway, Archibald MacLeish, Hart Crane, and Gertrude Stein, who would label them all the Lost Generation, Fitzgerald helped give voice to a feeling of rootlessness and discontent, ennui and fatigue that went beyond the mere letdown that always follows when the festivities come to an end. The ghostly silence that emerges after Gatsby's parties break up or the strange, disenchanted wanderings of Dick Diver at the end of *Tender* are symptomatic of a much more pervasive spiritual emptiness Fitzgerald found in the culture, and which we then find in his novels. Once a Rhodes scholar and a brilliant young psychiatrist, Diver says he cannot find the exact origins of his slow decline, and can say only that "The change came a long way back—but at first it didn't show. The manner remains intact for some time after the morale cracks." Echoing Amory Blaine's earlier declaration of his generation's radical liberation from all tradition, Fitzgerald has Dick say "[g]ood-by, my father—good-by, all my fathers," leaving him with little energy and emotional support to continue on as either a doctor or a husband.

It is a dim future, a vision that Nick Carraway describes as a "portentous, menacing road" that promises "a decade of loneliness . . . a thinning brief-case of enthusiasm," and one that expresses a lost generation's anxiety that in the aftermath of the Great War the belief in "eternal strength and health" and in "the essential goodness of people" were just "illusions of a nation" (*Tender* 117). Fitzgerald's novels suggest that if you were not one of the 200,000 who died in combat, then you were probably one of the millions of spiritual casualties.

Among many of the serious writers of Fitzgerald's day—Hemingway, Stein, William Faulkner, T.S. Eliot, Ezra Pound, and Wallace Stevens—writers who came to be the leading voices of American Modernism, there existed the sentiment that the culture was adrift and morally bankrupt. America had helped win the war, but lost its innocence in the process. And even before it lost its money in the crash, it had already lost its sense of direction. This sense of precariousness, coupled with Sigmund Freud's profoundly influential investigations into the unconscious, necessitated new modes of expression for Fitzgerald's contemporaries. To accurately capture this new sensibility, radical experiments in poetry and prose were undertaken, experiments that lend modernist literature its trademark intellectual rigor and introspection. Literary modernism employs an array of linguistic strategies in its attempt to communicate the harsh condition of modern life and the darknesses that linger in the individual psyche. In any modernist novel one is likely to encounter stream of conscious narration, the use of surreal images, the deployment of multiple narrators and shifting points of view, and the utilization of excessive repetition sometimes simply for the sense of sound and sometimes for no particular reason at all. More than just style, such strategies are meant to impart to the reader the experience of directionlessness, of nightmare, of the new century.

If these are the markers of a new literature in the 1920s, they are conspicuously absent from Fitzgerald's work. With the exception of the patchwork of images that convey to us Dick's courtship with the fragile Nicole in *Tender Is the Night*, one is hard pressed to find any extended experimental treatment of language in Fitzgerald's *oeuvre*. Even in *Tender* the exception might be explained by the novel's decidedly psychoanalytic subject matter. Though Fitzgerald did not, unlike his modernist counterparts, feel the need to break decisively with traditional prose forms, he still shared their feelings of despair, alienation, personal and social loss, and also, at times, their sense of liberation and excitement. Eschewing experimentation, Fitzgerald articulated his vision of modern life with a realistic prose style that aligned him with an older generation of writers of whom Mark Twain, William Dean Howells, and Edith Wharton are the most prominent practitioners. "The truthful treatment of material" was Howells's commission to the writers of his day, and it was a challenge that Fitzgerald met with his simple, transparent prose that, as good realism should, took for its subject the social life of the individual and the attendant questions of ethical conduct that come with living socially. Like the masters of realism that came before him, Fitzgerald aimed for, and struggled to maintain, an aura of objectivity that would allow him to first tease out the failings in his characters and then, if need be, to mete out their punishments.

Social realism was for Fitzgerald a manner of writing and judging that he would perfect in *The Great Gatsby* through the curious, insightful narrator Nick Carraway, who always maintains a certain amount of distance from his fascinating and mysterious neighbor. "Reserving judgments is a matter of infinite hope," claims Nick early in a novel that is about reservations, being reserved, being judgmental, and ultimately, about being judged. Fitzgerald's predominantly quiet and elegant prose stays focused in *The Great Gatsby* in a way that it does not in *This Side of Paradise*'s mishmash of genres or in *Tender Is the Night*, with its lack of a strong, governing consciousness. Dealing with alcoholism and mental instability, *Tender* too closely reflects Fitzgerald's own downfall into drinking, as well as his efforts to handle Zelda's breakdowns, for him to get the distance that makes *Gatsby* as lasting and memorable as it is. Likewise, Dick Diver finds that by being both a husband and a doctor to Nicole, objectivity becomes an impossible ideal. Playing both roles is "paralyzing [to] his faculties." He starts drinking a half-pint of alcohol a day; the book he had plan to write never gets finished. Despite its difficulties, to see incisively and honestly into the heart of a social situation or into the inner workings of one's self is Fitzgerald's desire, and is by extension, a desire of many of his leading characters. One of Nick Carraway's most cutting revelations at the end of the summer is his proclamation that at 30 he is "five years too old to lie to [himself] and call it honour." His voice sounds close to Fitzgerald's own. In contrast, Tom Buchanan will always remain myopic, will always choose to blame someone else first: "He [Gatsby] threw dust into your eyes," he tells Nick, "just like he did in Daisy's." And still others, such as Dick Diver, will avoid seeing the truth at all costs, as Fitzgerald suggests when Dick nearly loses his eyesight during his brawl with the taxi drivers. Even if *Tender* occasionally misses its mark because of its self-consciously autobiographical subject matter, it still evinces Fitzgerald's keen insight. His unencumbered prose, an instrument that is at times as precise as anything in Wharton or James, reveals to us what his characters sometimes cannot see for themselves.

Anyone who has read Fitzgerald of course knows that his writing has none of the dryness of a social scientist's. Even when it is most exacting, his

prose wells with empathy and the need for emotional release. Regarding
Fitzgerald's style, Milton Hindus perhaps said it best when he revealed that
"Fitzgerald's formula is to mix in a dash of romance with a liberal portion of
the most brutal realism and to drench the whole thing in irony." If
intellectually Fitzgerald is a realist, then he is also at heart a romantic in the
Keatsian tradition. It is from Keats that Fitzgerald not only borrows the line
for the title of *Tender Is the Night*, but it is to him that he also owes his entire
sensibility. Counterpointing Fitzgerald's biting social commentary on the
rich and the reckless are moments of intense poetic lyricism that unite him
with the Romantics and their belief that the sheer force of personal
emotional energy might be enough to transcend reality into the pure ideal.
We can see Amory Blaine's quest for authenticity in *This Side of Paradise* as
the opening salvo in Fitzgerald's lifelong struggle to move beyond the
machinations of the present moment and on into something more perfect,
thrilling, and perhaps unattainable, something he calls in *The Great Gatsby*
"the orgastic future that year by year recedes before us." Though Blaine
shows both his yearning and his adolescence in his grand gesture of
"stretch[ing] out his arms to the crystalline, radiant sky" as if it all belongs to
him, it is an image of longing that Fitzgerald would continue to employ
throughout his work. Our first glimpse of Gatsby in that romantic novel is of
him standing in the dark on his lawn looking up at the stars, trying "to
determine what share was his of our local heavens." It is a quiet moment of
dreaming for another world or another time that Gatsby repeats and that
comes to define him as a man with a "romantic readiness" and a "heightened
sensitivity to the promises of life," a phrase that could as easily and accurately
be applied to Fitzgerald himself.

Transcendentalism, the American offshoot of British Romanticism and
the school of thought that influenced Fitzgerald, looks to nature for evidence
of divine or ideal forms that might hold out the possibility for remaking the
world. For Emerson, the father of Transcendentalism, and for Thoreau, its
first son, the individual imagination with a "heightened sensitivity" could
unlock the transformative potential in nature's secrets. Preoccupied with the
world of the extravagantly rich and highly cultured, there is not much in
Fitzgerald's world that we would immediately recognize as natural in the
Emersonian sense. Yet Fitzgerald's powerful lyricism still participates, as do
his characters, in Emerson's artistic project of moving past the here-and-now,
what Fitzgerald calls "the foul dust," in order to attain a more attuned
consciousness beyond "the abortive sorrows and short-winded elations of
men" (*Gatsby* 6). For Emerson it is a project whose goal is an ideal realm, less
a physical place than it is a way of thinking that embraces change and fluidity.
In contrast, the ideal is often tangible for Fitzgerald. For Gatsby, it is a dream

that is most clearly emblematized in Daisy Buchanan who is so close that he can kiss her and yet forever out of reach in the distant past, a woman who is one moment in his mansion and in the next moment a world away on the other side of the water in East Egg. She is a young flapper, a flirt, his former lover, but she is also a spirit and a sprite who is "buoyed up as though upon an anchored balloon" (10). Gatsby strives not so much to remake the world by transcending it, though finally possessing his Daisy would surely mean this, but for a complete makeover of himself and his history. To change himself from James Gatz of North Dakota with few prospects in life to Jay Gatsby who lives in a house that is an "imitation of some Hôtel de Ville in Normandy," complete with "forty acres of lawn and garden," and an unobstructed view of the "the green light at the end of Daisy's dock" is a heroic effort and a romantic one, too. He "sprang from his Platonic conception of himself," writes Fitzgerald, a transformation not of the world of nature, but of the nature of man.

In a famous exchange with Hemingway, Fitzgerald remarked that "the very rich are different from us," to which Hemingway quipped back, "Yes, they have more money." Fitzgerald's observation is notable in that it reveals just how much he sometimes stood in awe of wealth and the admission it could buy, at least in Fitzgerald's view, to another world. While for Emerson the other world is a process, or a rapidly shifting state of mind, for Fitzgerald it is often a kind of stability that comes after a life of struggle, which has obvious connections to wealth and luxury. But money is more than a sign of wealth in Fitzgerald's work. It is an agent of change, the means by which one gets to the ideal. Money is ultimately much more useful for his characters for where it can take them, than for the things it can purchase. In Fitzgerald's novels, money may allow Gatsby a Rolls Royce and a swimming pool, provide Dexter Green of the 1922 short story "Winter Dreams" with "glittering things," and allow the Divers a villa in France, but more importantly it permits one to be in the presence of other people, people who otherwise seem unattainable, like Gatsby's Daisy, Green's Judy Jones, or Fitzgerald's own Zelda, who once broke off their engagement because of his small salary (*Babylon* 118). In the work of Fitzgerald, money loses its materiality and becomes the marker of grace, becomes the means by which one moves from this "less fashionable" world in order to settle in the idealized next one, even if the next one is only in East Egg (*Gatsby* 8).

Though the ideal world of the rich in Fitzgerald's novels is often mesmerizing, even breathtaking, it is subjected to a sound critique. By the end of his short stories, we often find that money is a poor guarantor of success, that is, if we think of success as something more than possessing "glittering things." In Fitzgerald, money gets one close to the dream, often figured as the woman of one's dreams, but in true Keatsian fashion, one never gets close enough to catch it, to catch her. Early on, Nick assures us that "Gatsby turned out all right at the end," but it is only later that we learn the terribly irony that Gatsby is preserved intact because he is floating dead in his pool on a "laden mattress" that, like the dream that sustained him, is still inflated. Apparently, nothing can puncture it. He is ever the dreamer, even in death. The lure of the ideal leads him to his watery grave. Despite all his wealth, Gatsby could only buy his way into brash West Egg and despite his nearly mythic struggle to refashion himself by recreating his own history, he will forever be in the eyes of East Egg's denizens "Mr. Nobody from Nowhere." Reminiscing about his failed courtship of Daisy, Gatsby believes that he is "going to fix everything just the way it was before," though Nick remains skeptical and Fitzgerald is unwavering in his conviction that some doors will remain forever closed no matter how much money one has.

To be called "Mr. Nobody from Nowhere" is a rebuke and an accusation that one is worthless regardless of how much one might be worth on paper. The charge echoes throughout Fitzgerald's novels. Just like Tom Buchanan's obsession with proper pedigrees, the Warrens are similarly suspicious of anyone without the obvious markers of class and distinction. "We don't know who you are," is Baby Warren's thinly veiled threat to Dick. Twelve years earlier in "Winter Dreams," the wealthy and fetching Judy Jones asked Dexter, "Who are you, anyhow," to which he limply responded, "I'm nobody" (*Babylon* 124). Questions about origins are found in most of Fitzgerald's fiction, and the answers given by his aspiring heroes are almost always the wrong ones. Undaunted, they still labor against the weight of the past, against feelings of belatedness, and against the often insurmountable hurdles of the future. Gatsby dies a "poor son-of-a-bitch," according to a former partygoer, an observation that has everything and nothing to do with money. Though still alive "in one town or another" at the conclusion of *Tender Is the Night*, Dick Diver is spiritually dead, drunken, divorced, and still questing after youth, this time in the guise of a "girl who worked in a grocery store." The man who repeatedly warned Nicole to "Control yourself!" is himself out of control. The Warren money had come with strings attached and when those strings are severed, Dick turns into a directionless marionette, nearly anonymous, a nobody. It is arguably a fate worse than Gatsby's.

"The tension between his inescapable commitment to the inner reality of his imagination and his necessary respect for the outer reality of the world," writes Fitzgerald's biographer Arthur Mizener, "is what gives his fiction its peculiar charm." The creative pull and push of his hard-nosed realist prose, his emotionally infused romantic lyricism, and his commitment to the idea that his characters "dreams" are mere mirages, are what in Mizener's purview lend Fitzgerald's best work "an air of enchantment that makes the most ordinary occasions haunting." In one shape or another, the novels of Fitzgerald are filled with ghosts and haunted landscapes. For Amory Blaine who only notices things that are "primarily beautiful: women, spring evenings, music at night, the sea," his "haunting" stems not only from his ability to imbue the world with the spirit of beauty, but more directly, it comes from his encounter with the ghost of Dick Humbird. Humbird's ghost is symbolic of the past's ability to haunt the present and is evidence that even for the generation that believes "all Gods [are] dead" those Gods, and the traditions they represent, still exert considerable influence. The wreckage of history cannot be easily swept away. Humbird's ghost reminds Amory of this, and reminds him too that he has a long journey ahead before he can honestly say, "I know myself," as he claims he does in the novel's final line. Unlike Dick's downward spiral, Amory in Fitzgerald's first and most optimistic novel moves upward, though his fate is still largely unwritten. Through the symbolic intrusions of the past, Fitzgerald hints that the future may be more shadowed with foreboding than glowing with "enchantment."

Revenants continue to materialize in other shapes in Fitzgerald's later fiction. For Gatsby, losing Daisy to Tom Buchanan causes the "city itself" to be "pervaded with a melancholy beauty." Likewise, Gatsby's own large spirit does not dissipate at death. "The East is haunted" for Nick after his friend's murder. In the 1931 short story "Babylon Revisited," Paris is "strange and portentous." Two years after the stock market crash, the city is the haunt of "ghosts from the past," such as Duncan Schaeffer and Lorraine Quarrles who continue their after-hours carousing even though the party is clearly over. For Charlie Wales, who is trying to recoup his losses and win back his daughter Honoria, all while fighting to stay sober, ghosts in the form of memories sweep over him "like a nightmare." *Tender Is the Night* picks up this same imagery and reworks it with greater psychological finesse. Nicole who cannot forget the nightmare of her incestuous encounter with her father, suffers from periodic breakdowns when confronted with moments of great anxiety. No literal ghost, the past is still a haunting presence for her. Though an entirely different cluster of fears motivates her, she is united with Gatsby who wants "to forget the sad thing that happened to me." The aura of "enchantment" that Mizener and others recognize in Fitzgerald's prose arises from its ability to straddle the line between this world and the next, a liminal space frequented by ghosts, people from the past, and the heartbreaking things one wishes to forget.

If Fitzgerald wished to forget any of his novels, it was probably *This Side of Paradise*. Upon publication, his inaugural book was not seen as an orderly, well-thematized work of literature. In an influential 1922 review that would in some ways haunt Fitzgerald, Edmund Wilson dismisses it as "illiterate" and "verging on the ludicrous." Wilson concluded that Fitzgerald's writing is "very immaturely imagined," and that his mind "suffers badly from lack of discipline and poverty of aesthetic ideas." *This Side of Paradise* is a messy novel, though the maturation of its protagonist does lend it a strong narrative arc that helps shape its clutter and contain its moments of wildness. With the benefit of hindsight, *This Side of Paradise* also can be seen as articulating a hornet's nest of concerns—the proper route to self-transformation, the role of past traditions in a new century, the corrupting influence of money, the pitfalls of youthful excess—that organize all of Fitzgerald's later work. But Wilson's central contention though was that Fitzgerald's work lacked order not because he was an immature writer, but because he was an emotional one. In his view, Fitzgerald's first novel was missing the intricate patterning of symbols and gestures that hold a work of art together, that give it density, its intellectual stringency, and its staying power. Ezra Pound, Fitzgerald's modernist colleague, urged writers to make use of the "Image"—a radical condensation of an emotional or intellectual problem in the form of a visual expression—so that their work might resonate with meaning on multiple levels while still being economical with language. Such "Images" are absent from Fitzgerald's fictional world in Wilson's estimation, yet with the benefit of peering back over his entire career we can see that even in this 1920 novel Fitzgerald is beginning to work with a ghostly tableaux that he invokes with more success, and more nuance in his mature fiction.

Critics writing after Wilson, especially those publishing after Fitzgerald's death in 1940, are able to survey and evaluate his entire literary output, from *This Side of Paradise* to the incomplete, but promising, *The Last Tycoon*. And unlike Wilson in 1922, they have the gift of *Gatsby*. *The Great Gatsby* was critically well received in 1925, despite its mediocre sales, and throughout the 1920s Fitzgerald was lauded as a serious and popular novelist and as the good-looking poster boy of a generation maturing in the healthy glow of postwar prosperity. But his standing among critics went into freefall in the late 1930s when writing about the exploits of the wealthy seemed irresponsible in a time of burdening and bludgeoning poverty. It was up to Fitzgerald scholars working in the 1940s and '50s to resurrect Fitzgerald's nearly dead reputation. They exhumed him in part with the highly refined tools of New Criticism that was coming to prominence in the American academy in the years immediately after World War II. With its rigorous emphasis on the close investigation of a work's images, structure, and style, and with its preference for morally ambiguous literature, New Criticism provided a framework and a lens for reevaluating Fitzgerald's novels. The 'missing' symbols of *This Side of Paradise* were uncovered. Even more of them were found in *Gatsby*, which also possesses an impressive narrative cohesion that New Critics admire. In a 1945 appreciation entitled "F. Scott Fitzgerald," Lionel Trilling calls the "form" of *The Great Gatsby* "ingenious—with the ingenuity, however, not of craft but of intellectual intensity." The focus on Fitzgerald's intellectual acumen was a radical departure from earlier critics. It is not *Gatsby*'s emotional heft that gives it the "weight and relevance . . . of very few American books of its time." It is its form and its use of "ideographs," Trilling's equivalent to Pound's "Image." For examples Trilling points to "the ideographic use that is made of the Washington Heights flat, the terrible 'valley of ashes' seen from the Long Island Railroad, Gatsby's incoherent parties, and the huge sordid eyes of the oculist's advertising sign. To Trilling's catalog, one might add Fitzgerald's symbolic use of color—the white that ironically connotes Daisy's innocence, the red color of the "jewels, chiefly rubies" which reappears as Myrtle's and Gatsby's spilt blood, the green light on Daisy's dock mimicking the color of money—or the novel's interplay of lights and darks, or the symbolic dust that not only typifies life in the "valley of ashes" but is everywhere, even in Gatsby's mansion. For Trilling, whose status as one of the preeminent critics of his generation helped resuscitate Fitzgerald's standing in the American canon of literature, these images come together to create the "ideal voice" for a "book [which] grows in weight of significance with the years." By regarding him as a writer of "intellectual intensity," Trilling counters Wilson's allegation that Fitzgerald is primarily a writer of the heart, one with emotional plentitude, but suffering from a "poverty of aesthetic ideas." Instead of the odd-man-out among the other intellectual writers of his generation, Trilling sees Fitzgerald crafting in his novels a grand design, a system of thought that aligns him more with his fellow modern American writers than his intense lyricism at first reveals.

Taking cues from Carl Jung's theory of archetypes, much modernist literature exhibits an interest in mythologies—the most ancient of grand designs—which hold forth the possibility of articulating alternative ways of behaving and surviving in the world. In their original guises, modernist writers deemed older mythologies as irrelevant in an age when "all Gods [were] dead, all wars fought." But when retooled as new art, they could provide order, even solace, to a generation mired in the spiritual vacuum and ennui of the years between the world wars. Even when the past and its attendant mythologies met with ironic treatment at the hands of modernists—James Joyce's *Ulysses* is the paramount example—such work could powerfully communicate the utopian longings of a lost aesthetic ideal.

For Trilling and for many readers of Fitzgerald, the grand design or the mythopoetics that underlie his best novel are intimately tied to the founding mythologies of America. Trilling writes, "For Gatsby . . . comes inevitably to stand for America itself. Ours is the only nation that prides itself upon a dream and gives its name to one, 'the American dream'." The assurance among the first European settlers in America that they could fashion a new world, one without the corrupting influence of European ideologies and legacies, one that sprang from a "Platonic conception" of itself, and that with the potent mix of Providence and hard work could not fail to succeed, is a national fantasy that reverberates through the dreams of Jay Gatsby. Gatsby is the quintessential American success story, a fictionalized tale of 'rags-to-riches.' By modeling himself upon Benjamin Franklin's "Thirteen Names of Virtues" and following a similar schedule of self-improvement, the adolescent James Gatz, the son of "shiftless and unsuccessful farm people," the "penniless young man without a past," subscribes to the notion that through study, thrift, and kindness he can transform himself into the fashionable, wealthy, and handsome playboy named Jay Gatsby. Like the early "Dutch sailors' eyes," which Nick imagines took in the "fresh, green breast of the new world" with wonder, so too does Gatsby stare in hopeful amazement at possibilities afforded by life. It is a look that is symbolized most cogently when Gatsby gazes at Daisy's "green" light. At the end of her dock Gatsby sees the potential for future happiness, acceptance, and the resumption of a stalled love. It also reminds him of a perfectly preserved moment of their past courtship. Yet invariably it means more. For the reader of the novel, Gatsby's personal past carries all the weight of the nation's 'discovery.'

The story of Gatsby's rise is the story of a nation in love with progress, with movement, with "run[ning] faster, stretch[ing] out our arms farther" toward the "the green light, the orgastic future." Gatsby stands as an American archetype, a fictionalized Horatio Alger that according to Trilling "should turn" "our mind . . . to the thought of the nation," just as Nick's mind contemplates "our identity with this country for one strange hour." While recognizing the durable force and lure of America's self-fashioning individualism, its promise of financial wealth, of love and of spiritual grace, Fitzgerald also recognizes the costs of such an unwavering pursuit. He sternly reports that Gatsby "paid a high price for living too long with a single dream." With its naivety and blind ambition, Gatsby's dream is the kind "a seventeen year old boy would be likely to invent," a comment by Nick that links Gatsby with Amory Blaine. But Gatsby is also dogged by nightmares of the past that "haunted him in his bed at night," a haunting that suggests that despite the inexorable will of a nation or an individual that it is impossible to "return to a certain starting place" again. Failing to realize this is Gatsby's fatal flaw, his hubris. Twenty-five years into the twentieth century, Fitzgerald suggests that it is already too late for surprise. His characters are often cynical and bored—"I've been everywhere and seen everything and done everything," frets Daisy—and instead of migrating west to reinvent life, they all head to the old and corrupted East. Nick, the Buchanans, and Gatsby know the frontier is closed. Showing the influence of T.S. Eliot, Fitzgerald has Doctor T.J. Eckleburg's eyes ponder a wasteland of modernity. These are God's eyes, worn down, dimmed to the point of needing spectacles. Lacking color and energy, the world is hard to look at anymore. In the lyrical passages that close out *The Great Gatsby*, the vision of America shimmers for only "a transitory enchanted moment." The feeling is one of belatedness. It was "the last time in history" when man was "face to face . . . with something commensurate to his capacity for wonder" (140). Even before he set out to win back Daisy, Gatsby's dream, like the American Dream, "was already behind him, somewhere back in that vast obscurity beyond the city, where the dark fields of the republic rolled on under the night." Gatsby set foot on the shores of Long Island hundreds of years behind schedule.

If Lionel Trilling sees Fitzgerald as a novelist reworking enduring national themes, then Malcolm Cowley in his 1956 retrospective essay "Fitzgerald: The Romance of Money" treats him as a writer firmly entrenched in the peculiar milieu of the 1920s. In Cowley's view Fitzgerald is a finely attuned storyteller living in a time when "[m]anners and morals were changing." Adding support to Cowley's claims, Fitzgerald himself announced that "'America was going on the greatest, gaudiest spree in history and there was going to be plenty to tell about it'". With an ear for jazz and a nose for drink, Cowley's Fitzgerald is a man of his time, though he quickly adds that Fitzgerald "lived harder than most people have ever lived and acted out his dreams with an extraordinary intensity of emotion." Coming after the New Critical studies with their sole emphasis on the work of art itself, Cowley's essay, along with Arthur Mizener's *The Far Side of Paradise* and Milton Stern's *The Golden Moment*, looks to the colorful and tragic events of Fitzgerald's life and uses them to stress the inextricability of biography and art. Amory Blaine, notes Cowley, "looks and talks like Fitzgerald; they read "the same books" and fall in love with "the same girls." Fitzgerald speaks for his young contemporaries who "had a sense of reckless confidence not only about money but about life in general," and more specifically, he gives a voice to the "masculine ideal of the 1920s," the "'entire man in the Goethe-Byron-Shaw tradition, with an opulent American touch,'" the sort of man who lives with "'an utter disregard of consequences.'" Of course Fitzgerald's writing is in the end preoccupied with consequences: the dissolution of Anthony Patch, the death of Gatsby, Dick Diver's headlong dive "into a lifeless mass," Fitzgerald's own crack-up. Cowley is right to label the code of conduct exhibited by Fitzgerald's men as a "masculine *ideal*." Whether American or masculine, the pursuit of ideals in Fitzgerald's work always leads to some kind of wreck; the smash-ups seemed particularly bad in the 1920s, the first generation that learned to drive.

Studies that take into account both Fitzgerald's life and his writing are powerful in part for their ability to cast Fitzgerald himself as an exemplar of a particularly American brand of tragedy. In such work the implication is often that Fitzgerald is even more archetypal than Gatsby. He "strove to achieve in the actual world the ideal life he could so vividly imagine," explains Mizener. Even though Fitzgerald recognized the pitfalls of turning one's aesthetic contemplation of the American Dream into a lived reality, he tried to meet the challenge anyway. Torn between what America could be in his imagination and what it really was, between his own thirst for money and his competing desire to be a first-rate novelist who had some serious critiques of America that he wanted to share, Fitzgerald, in the opinion of his biographical critics, was destined to suffer. Suffering was not thought of as detrimental to his art; on the contrary, such critics treated it as the fuel that energized his writing. "Without question," Stern asserts in *The Golden Moment*, "Zelda's emotional collapse provided material for the final version of *Tender Is the Night*," an assertion backed up by Fitzgerald's revelation to Zelda that he was not sure if they were real anymore or if they were characters in his novel (Stern 292). The parallels between Fitzgerald's tempestuous marriage and *Tender* are clear to anyone even scantly familiar with both. But Stern's premise centers on a greater assertion than the biographical inflections that arguably may be found in any one passage or another. For Stern, Fitzgerald's suffering was heroic. In granting Fitzgerald the aura of heroism, Stern mythologizes him. His dissipation into alcoholism, his long 'unproductive' years between his two mature novels, and his time writing unsuccessful screenplays in Hollywood all embody for Stern more than the life of just one man. Concluding his discussion of *Tender Is the Night*, Stern graciously labels Fitzgerald "one of the most 'American' writers," who "capture[s] greatly the peculiarities of [his] national experience," and in doing so touches "all men everywhere." The novel that originates in the troubled marriage of a particular man in a particular time takes on national significance and then international or universal appeal.

In response to critics who read the history of 1920s America through the paradigmatic life of F. Scott Fitzgerald, recent scholars have returned to his work to look less for evidence of the man and more for insight into the workings of the culture itself. For academics such as Ronald Berman and Walter Benn Michaels, Fitzgerald's life during the Jazz Age is not approached as one that is "at once representative and dramatic," nor is the moral of his personal history treated as "the teasing puzzle of any human history" (Mizener 1). Berman's 1994 examination *The Great Gatsby and Modern Times* in particular situates Fitzgerald's novel within the context of early twentieth-century pop culture, with a special accent upon the new expressions of identity that were made possible by the era's revolutions in mass production and the proliferation of venues for mass marketing. Magazines with wide circulations like *Vanity Fair, Reader's Digest*, and the *Saturday Evening Post* enticed readers with pages of advertisements. Large factories pumped out 27 million automobiles by 1929, making this former luxury a middle-class staple. An array of products, from designer clothing to washing machines, which had once been solely the domain of the elite, flooded the market at lower prices. More so than any prior moment in American history, the expansive economy of the 1920s gave the impression that liberation from the constraints of time and class required little more than an afternoon shopping in one of New York's block-long department stores.

Commenting on *The Great Gatsby*, Berman notes, "The language of the marketplace infiltrates everywhere. . . . Myrtle buys her dog and Tom buys Myrtle. Nick rents, Gatsby buys, the Buchanans inherit." In an age saturated with marketing and a time when the recent inventions of radio and film proffered style and promised love, it only makes sense for Daisy to tell Gatsby, "You resemble the advertisement of the man . . . You know the advertisement of the man." Taken together, Myrtle's collection of scandal magazines, her elaborate dresses, Gatsby's colorful and expensive shirts and suits that cause Daisy to croon, his old yachting costume, his hydroplane, these are all indicative of a distinctly modern sensibility that sees identity as something malleable or artificial, or at the very least, as something commercial. In the postwar marketplace, the aisles were crowded with makeup and ready-to-wear clothing and women in bobbed hairdos with disposable incomes. New identities could be bought, old ones updated or replaced. The flapper was the media darling, both carefree and corporate. Trying to mimic the sauntering insouciance of this new icon, Myrtle buys into the logic of consumerist culture. She believes that with a change of clothes she can leave the valley of ashes behind for the life of a Manhattan socialite. Gatsby's appropriations of the market's potential for magical transformation are even grander. Thinking of himself primarily as a consumer, he banks his hopes on the belief that the right possessions—a new name, a new self—will win him Daisy, though the keen reader almost certainly senses he is mistaken.

Though Berman's study is confined to Fitzgerald's most esteemed novel, mercenary themes extend to Fitzgerald's later work, especially *Tender is the Night*, which even more than *Gatsby* is a book about buying and selling people and dreams. Rosemary, around whom many of these concerns cluster, unabashedly sees herself as "property" that might be traded, owned by another, or kept to herself. From the "middle of the middle class," however, she also was raised with "the idea of work," and was warned early by her mother that "economically you're a boy, not a girl." If she is going to succeed in the American economy she must acquire as well as be acquired. With little savings to call her own, her mother hires her out to Hollywood and then sanctions her pursuit of Dick Diver for the experience and money it might bring. Consumer, purchaser, and laborer, Rosemary is at the crux of the novel's questions about how a woman might transform herself in order to survive in the marketplace without the benefit of inherited wealth. *Tender's* other leading woman, Nicole, also considers herself "valuable property," though it is largely on account of her fragility, and not from economic necessity, that she feels required to advertise her charms. Her older sister has none of the pressure of securing a husband and a doctor in one deal. On the verge of revealing to Dick the "big houses she lived in," Nicole remembers, "there was no home left to her, save emptiness and pain." The market's promise of "glittering things," Fitzgerald intimates, is usually just gold dust in the eyes.

In a boom-time economy Fitzgerald's characters "do what all Americans are encouraged to do," observes Berman. They buy low. They sell high. They trade-up. To become someone else, someone better, more beautiful, more wealthy, or more free is, of course, one of the perennial aspirations in American mythology. Berman, like earlier critics, sees *Gatsby* as tapping into a distinctly American set of morals and concerns that stress hard work and upward mobility. There is, however, nothing inherently truthful or ideal in these values, according to Berman. They emanate not from 'another world,' but from a particular economic system where money, not Keatsian Beauty, is the bottom line. The desire for material and class advancement in Fitzgerald's novels must be squared against his acute awareness that American society is held in check by class boundaries that will not budge or be bridged. The marketplace's assurance of self-transformation is a chimera that both Berman and Fitzgerald decry. Eventually one gets "smashed up" by others who, like the elite Buchanans, will not accept one's illusions. When Fitzgerald's men and women "falsif[y] . . . their individual lives," Berman argues it reflects a much larger falsification of ideas." The extent to which "we [can] construct our own identities" is limited to "our theatrical abilities" and limited by "our natural enemies." Myrtle's role as a sophisticate is not believable; brought back from Manhattan to die in the dust of working-class Queens, she is a victim of the Buchanans' ruthless instinct for self-preservation. Jordan Baker escapes, but only by remaining "incurably dishonest" and detached. The consummate performer, Gatsby still would have never been accepted in East Egg. And Nick, no longer able to act the part of an Easterner, returns home disappointed. In *Tender* we find a similar mix of winners and losers, though everyone loses something. Dick has almost nothing at the end, not even self-respect. Nicole's "valuable property" is transferred to Tommy Barban, the man who is everything Dick is not. Of all of Fitzgerald's characters, perhaps Rosemary holds the most promise. A combination of determination and savvy keeps her alive. When we last see her in a conversation about acting, Fitzgerald hints that she may be enough of a chameleon to survive and enough of a romantic to remain forever human, forever in trouble.

Ultimately Fitzgerald's novels may belong to his characters with working-class and middle-class origins. But they are also stories about the concerns of America's wealthiest. The expansive economy of the 1920s meant that the accoutrements of wealth were available to more people than ever before, a change that generated anxiety among the nation's elite and led them to shore up their class boundaries by reinforcing the importance of heritage and breeding. Owning the right possessions was one thing, but having the right past, which could not be bought, was another matter entirely. A middle-class social climber might try to appear affluent, but only America's oldest families could claim proprietary rights to a proper legacy. The era's promise of social mobility was met with a concomitant solidification of both class and racial barriers by the elevation of ancestry over wealth itself, a strategy for keeping out the 'undesirable.' And it was fueled largely by an anxiety over 'purity' that Walter Benn Michaels traces not only through Fitzgerald's writing, but through much of the modernist period's literature.

Gatsby's "desire for a different future," notes Michaels in the historicist study *Our America*, is a "desire for a different past . . . a matter of 'ancestors.'" Yet regardless of how much one might try, in Fitzgerald's world the past is never erased. There is always a Tom Buchanan to investigate it, or a hapless and dismayed father to show up at one's funeral. For snobs and racists such as Tom Buchanan, Gatsby's wish to marry upward is conflated with racial miscegenation, and so has implications beyond class politics. For a man "from Nowhere" to dream of a properly bred woman like Daisy is, in Tom's mind, equivalent to an "intermarriage between black and white." The blurring of class and race lines for Tom is evidence that "Civilization's going to pieces," an inflammatory claim that he reinforces with the book he touts to everyone, "'The Rise of the Coloured Empires." Michaels tracks down Tom's allusion to the polemics of real-life racist Lothrop Stoddard, author of *The Rising Tide of Color* (1920), and places it within the context of the national argument in the 1920s over limiting the immigration that was changing, to the fear of some, the face of the American citizenry. For the established families in Fitzgerald's novels, such as the Buchanans, or the Warrens who are listed among "the great feudal families" of Chicago, there was much at stake in preserving the traditional markers of identity. Mass marketing was akin to mass immigration in that both might let 'outsiders' 'in.' Hence Meyer Wolfshiem, Gatsby's Jewish business associate remains a peripheral, shadowy character, much like Gatsby himself. While Dick may hold center stage in *Tender*, the Warrens make clear that the son of a clergyman will have to be pushed out of the family eventually. The world that Gatsby contemplates as he gazes at the green light demarcating the Buchanan property is one to which he is not wanted. Staying in his place in West Egg is what, for the Buchanans, keeps their world pure and ideal.

More generally though, it is not just the world of America's aristocrats that is in danger of becoming sullied. The whole world is impure for Fitzgerald. Its soiled condition stems from a malaise and decay that is more widespread than even the conservatives of Fitzgerald's day would admit. Even at the outset of his career, Fitzgerald has Amory Blaine indict all of humanity with his vivid description of "dirty restaurants where careless, tired people helped themselves to sugar with their own coffee-spoons, leaving hard brown deposits in the bowl." Amory sees among the poor "only coarseness, physical filth, and stupidity." The rich are equally "corrupt." Like Hollywood in *The Last Tycoon*, in *This Side of Paradise* Broadway is the site of so many dreams, yet Amory takes in little besides its dirt and noise. Spurned in one way or another by Isabelle, Rosalind, and Eleanor, he sinks into a depression in which all of humanity is fetid and impoverished. We might be tempted to dismiss his sourness and melancholia as the egotism of adolescence if the attitude were not as pervasive as it is throughout Fitzgerald's work.

Two years later, Fitzgerald's readers would watch the fall of the young stars, Gloria and Anthony Patch, in his follow-up novel *The Beautiful and Damned*. In love with physical beauty, they are consequently fixated on aging. Though vain and frequently unlikable, the Patches, like most characters in Fitzgerald's fiction, are interesting expressions of his thematic concerns with decay and corruption. They have destroyed their own lives and ruined Shuttleworth's, but there is still pathos to be found in watching Gloria sink to the floor distraught and whimpering "Oh, I don't want to live without my pretty face! Oh, what's *happened*?" "[A] bleak and disordered wreck" at 32, Anthony evokes Nick's fear of "the portentous, menacing road of a new decade" in *The Great Gatsby*, which is exactly what being in his thirties means for Dick in *Tender*. When Anthony slips into a kind of second childhood, it is his retreat from the real world into innocence, though in Fitzgerald such a respite from the polluted world of adulthood is bound to be short-lived. "[S]ort of dyed and unclean" at the end, these characters touch a nerve in a world where people can be, and often are, both beautiful and damned.

To see life as more unclean than clean, more decayed than fresh, and more impure than pure is to see the human condition in existential terms. Present in Fitzgerald's earliest work, it is a tone that became darker the more he wrote. Alluding to the years right after the war when Fitzgerald did his best writing, Malcolm Cowley reflects that "[a] word then frequently applied to the younger men was 'disillusioned.'" Disbelieving the grand promises of their leaders "[y]oung men turned away from social aims," Cowley continues, "and from any type of public service" and concentrated on their own pursuit of pleasure and their own art. But even in turning inward, Fitzgerald and others of the Lost Generation did not shirk their engagement with the world. In their art the world is very much on display and on trial. It is judged to be dishonest, diseased, and decaying. In *The Great Gatsby* Fitzgerald offers just such a critique, and he does so with a force he never achieved again. The seemingly carefree world of Long Island's wealthy enclaves, Fitzgerald notes, is a short car ride from the valley of ashes in Queens. They are both funereal, covered with dust, and like the whole world, they are wastelands. Driving into Manhattan with Gatsby, Nick thinks of the city as a "wild promise of all the mystery and beauty in the world." Then a hearse passes them by, a *memento mori* of the omnipresent shadow of death, and a foreshadowing of the "death car" that drives through this novel. Surrounded by death and dissolution, his characters cannot help but feel older than they really are. "If we were young we'd rise and dance," laments Daisy, who is of course still far from old age. She speaks instead of her generation's fatigue from its relentless effort to hide its spiritual vacancy beneath the sounds of song and celebration. The music eventually stops at Gatsby's mansion. The last time Nick sees him alive, he tells him that the Buchanans and their friends are a "rotten crowd" and that he's "worth the whole damn bunch put together." Nick prides himself on his compliment, but the careful reader realizes that Nick has just told Gatsby that he is only worth as much as a whole crowd of "rotten" people. The "obscene word, scrawled by some boy" on the steps of Gatsby's house is the verdict of the next generation that will rise up after Fitzgerald's has finished squandering its prosperity.

One encouraging face of that next generation is Rosemary, though in *Tender Is the Night* she is hardly a fiery social critic. In the impure world of Fitzgerald's novels, she has a refreshing *je ne sais quoi*. Ebullient, independent, and only 18 when the story begins, she is already a keen observer of the people around her. She is aware of the triangulation of desire that develops between her, Dick, and Nicole, and she is equally aware of how to make a graceful exit. In a novel in which sexuality is primarily a source of pain and corruption, Rosemary seems in control, makes her own choices, and if she is a bit infatuated with Dick Diver, it brings her no lasting harm. The situation is different for others around her. Most tragically, Devereux Warren commits incest with his daughter and then commits her to a psychiatric clinic when she exhibits symptoms of schizophrenia. Dick, in turn, becomes her caretaker, her father figure. His own affair with Rosemary, half his age and the star of *Daddy's Girl*, also has strong incestuous overtones, though Rosemary knows when to keep her distance and when to love on her own terms. As the novel proceeds, problems with intimacy and power begin to pile up. Dick is accused of improper sexual conduct with a young patient; later, he is mistaken for a man who has raped a five-year-old and he even takes a perverse pleasure in admitting to it; at the end, he is entangled with a "girl . . . in a grocery store." What these relationships amount to for Fitzgerald is the feeling that the private love between two people can be as damaging and tawdry as any of the social corruptions that pervade this novel with its wide, international concerns.

Having said "good-by" to the values of "honor, courtesy, and courage" that sustained the generation of his father, a generation born in the earlier, simpler century, Dick more than ever needs "to be loved" by the youth who will soon replace him. *Tender Is the Night* is a book about many kinds of love, some of them criminal, some of them just insecure, but it is chiefly a story about an older, tired generation's love of a younger generation's vitality and promise. As much a late-night reveler as anyone in *Gatsby*, Dick exclaims early on, "I want to give a really *bad* party." As he ages he looks more and more to the young, especially Rosemary, to replace his spent energy. Dick may trust that their vigor will cure his "Black Death," but late in his writing career Fitzgerald knows that the idealization of youth is no solution to disillusionment. The novel ends the summer before the October crash, portending that things will get much worse before they get better.

If there is to be anything redeemed from the smashed lives in Fitzgerald's work, it is up to the generations of future readers who come not so much seeking answers, but examples of the moments when the dreams turn nasty or when the parties go bad. Sensitive readers can learn from Fitzgerald what it means to see the world romantically, but also what it means to stare at it when it is ugly and not to blink, not to dodge responsibilities, to look hard at "what a grotesque thing a rose is" and refuse to go back home. To "run faster, stretch out our arms farther" while not succumbing to the "illusions of a nation" is Fitzgerald's cautious advice to his readers. And if the future is elusive, "that's no matter" for soon it will be "one fine morning."

The Liberal Imagination

" 'So be it! I die content and my destiny is fulfilled,' said Racine's Orestes; and there is more in his speech than the insanely bitter irony that appears on the surface. Racine, fully conscious of this tragic grandeur, permits Orestes to taste for a moment before going mad with grief the supreme joy of a hero; to assume his *exemplary* role." The heroic awareness of which André Gide speaks in his essay on Goethe was granted to Scott Fitzgerald for whatever grim joy he might find in it. It is a kind of seal set upon his heroic quality that he was able to utter his vision of his own fate publicly and aloud and in *Esquire* with no lessening of his dignity, even with an enhancement of it. The several essays in which Fitzgerald examined his life in crisis have been gathered together by Edmund Wilson—who is for many reasons the most appropriate editor possible—and published, together with Fitzgerald's notebooks and some letters, as well as certain tributes and memorabilia, in a volume called, after one of the essays, *The Crack-Up*. It is a book filled with the grief of the lost and the might-have-been, with physical illness and torture of mind. Yet the heroic quality is so much here, Fitzgerald's assumption of the "exemplary role" is so proper and right that it occurs to us to say, and not merely as a piety but as the most accurate expression of what we really do feel, that

"F. Scott Fitzgerald", from The Liberal Imagination by Lionel Trilling ©1950 by Lionel Trilling. Reprinted by permission.

Nothing is here for tears, nothing to wail
Or knock the breast, no weakness, no contempt,
Dispraise, or blame, nothing but well and fair,
And what may quiet us in a death so noble.

This isn't what we may fittingly say on all tragic occasions, but the original occasion for these words has a striking aptness to Fitzgerald. Like Milton's Samson, he had the consciousness of having misused the power with which he had been endowed. "I had been only a mediocre caretaker . . . of my talent," he said. And the parallel carries further, to the sojourn among the Philistines and even to the maimed hero exhibited and mocked for the amusement of the crowd—on the afternoon of September 25, 1936, the New York Evening Post carried on its front page a feature story in which the triumphant reporter tells how he managed to make his way into the Southern nursing home where the sick and distracted Fitzgerald was being cared for and there "interviewed" him, taking all due note of the contrast between the present humiliation and the past glory. It was a particularly gratuitous horror, and yet in retrospect it serves to augment the moral force of the poise and fortitude which marked Fitzgerald's mind in the few recovered years that were left to him.

The root of Fitzgerald's heroism is to be found, as it sometimes is in tragic heroes, in his power of love. Fitzgerald wrote much about love, he was preoccupied with it as between men and women, but it is not merely where he is being explicit about it that his power appears. It is to be seen where eventually all a writer's qualities have their truest existence, in his style. Even in Fitzgerald's early, cruder books, or even in his commercial stories, and even when the style is careless, there is a tone and pitch to the sentences which suggest his warmth and tenderness, and, what is rare nowadays and not likely to be admired, his gentleness without softness. In the equipment of the moralist and therefore in the equipment of the novelist, aggression plays an important part, and although it is of course sanctioned by the novelist's moral intention and by whatever truth of moral vision he may have, it is often none the less fierce and sometimes even cruel. Fitzgerald was a moralist to the core and his desire to "preach at people in some acceptable form" is the reason he gives for not going the way of Cole Porter and Rogers and Hart—we must always remember in judging him how many real choices he was free and forced to make—and he was gifted with the satiric eye; yet we feel that in his morality he was more drawn to celebrate the good than to denounce the bad. We feel of him, as we cannot feel of all moralists, that he did not attach himself to the good because this attachment would sanction his fierceness toward the bad—his first impulse was to love the good, and we know this the more surely because we perceive that he loved the good not only with his mind but also with his quick senses and his youthful pride and desire.

He really had but little impulse to blame, which is the more remarkable because our culture peculiarly honors the act of blaming, which it takes as the sign of virtue and intellect. "Forbearance, good word," is one of the jottings in his notebook. When it came to blame, he preferred, it seems, to blame himself. He even did not much want to blame the world. Fitzgerald knew where "the world" was at fault. He knew that it was the condition, the field, of tragedy. He is conscious of "what preyed on Gatsby, what foul dust floated in the wake of his dreams." But he never made out that the world imposes tragedy, either upon the heroes of his novels, whom he called his "brothers," or upon himself. When he speaks of his own fate, he does indeed connect it with the nature of the social world in which he had his early flowering, but he never finally lays it upon that world, even though at the time when he was most aware of his destiny it was fashionable with minds more pretentious than his to lay all personal difficulty whatever at the door of the "social order." It is, he feels, *his* fate—and as much as to anything else in Fitzgerald, we respond to the delicate tension he maintained between his idea of personal free will and his idea of circumstance: we respond to that moral and intellectual energy. "The test of a first-rate intelligence," he said, "is the ability to hold two opposed ideas in the mind, at the same time, and still retain the ability to function."

The power of love in Fitzgerald, then, went hand in hand with a sense of personal responsibility and perhaps created it. But it often happens that the tragic hero can conceive and realize a love that is beyond his own prudence or beyond his powers of dominance or of self-protection, so that he is destroyed by the very thing that gives him his spiritual status and stature. From Proust we learn about a love that is destructive by a kind of corrosiveness, but from Fitzgerald's two mature novels, *The Great Gatsby* and *Tender Is the Night*, we learn about a love—perhaps it is peculiarly American—that is destructive by reason of its very tenderness. It begins in romance, sentiment, even "glamour"—no one, I think, has remarked how innocent of mere "sex," how charged with sentiment is Fitzgerald's description of love in the jazz age—and it takes upon itself reality, and permanence, and duty discharged with an almost masochistic scrupulousness of honor. In the bright dreams begins the responsibility which needs so much prudence and dominance to sustain; and Fitzgerald was anything but a prudent man and he tells us that at a certain point in his college career "some old desire for personal dominance was broken and gone." He connects that loss of desire for dominance with his ability to write; and he set down in his notebook the belief that "to record one must be unwary." Fitzgerald, we may say, seemed to feel that both love and art needed a sort of personal defenselessness.

The phrase from Yeats, the derivation of the "responsibility" from the "dreams," reminds us that we must guard against dismissing, with easy words about its immaturity, Fitzgerald's preoccupation with the bright charm of his youth. Yeats himself, a wiser man and wholly fulfilled in his art, kept to the last of his old age his connection with his youthful vanity. A writer's days must be bound each to each by his sense of his life, and Fitzgerald the undergraduate was father of the best in the man and the novelist.

His sojourn among the philistines is always much in the mind of everyone who thinks about Fitzgerald, and indeed it was always much in his own mind. Everyone knows the famous exchange between Fitzgerald and Ernest Hemingway—Hemingway refers to it in his story, "The Snows of Kilimanjaro" and Fitzgerald records it in his notebook—in which, to Fitzgerald's remark, "The very rich are different from us," Hemingway replied, "Yes, they have more money." It is usually supposed that Hemingway had the better of the encounter and quite settled the matter. But we ought not be too sure. The novelist of a certain kind, if he is to write about social life, may not brush away the reality of the differences of class, even though to do so may have the momentary appearance of a virtuous social avowal. The novel took its rise and its nature from the radical revision of the class structure in the eighteenth century, and the novelist must still live by his sense of class differences, and must be absorbed by them, as Fitzgerald was, even though he despise them, as Fitzgerald did.

No doubt there was a certain ambiguity in Fitzgerald's attitude toward the "very rich"; no doubt they were for him something more than the mere object of his social observation. They seem to have been the nearest thing to an aristocracy that America could offer him, and we cannot be too simple about what a critic has recently noted, the artist's frequent "taste for aristocracy, his need—often quite open—of a superior social class with which he can make some fraction of common cause—enough, at any rate, to account for his own distinction." Every modern reader is by definition wholly immune from all ignoble social considerations, and, no matter what his own social establishment or desire for it may be, he knows that in literature the interest in social position must never be taken seriously. But not all writers have been so simple and virtuous—what are we to make of those risen gentlemen, Shakespeare and Dickens, or those fabricators of the honorific "de," Voltaire and Balzac? Yet their snobbery—let us call it that— is of a large and generous kind and we are not entirely wrong in connecting their peculiar energies of mind with whatever it was they wanted from gentility or aristocracy. It is a common habit of writers to envision an actuality of personal life which shall have the freedom and the richness of detail and the order of form that they desire in art. Yeats, to mention him again, spoke of the falseness of the belief that the "inherited glory of the rich" really holds richness of life. This, he said, was a mere dream; and yet, he goes on, it is a necessary illusion—

> Yet Homer had not sung
> Had he not found it certain beyond dreams
> That out of life's own self-delight had sprung
> The abounding glittering jet. . . .

And Henry James, at the threshold of his career, allegorized in his story "Benvolio" the interplay that is necessary for some artists between their creative asceticism and the bright, free, gay life of worldliness, noting at the same time the desire of worldliness to destroy the asceticism.[1]

With a man like Goethe the balance between the world and his asceticism is maintained, and so we forgive him his often absurd feelings— but perhaps absurd as well as forgivable only in the light of our present opinion of his assured genius—about aristocracy. Fitzgerald could not always keep the balance true; he was not, as we know, a prudent man. And no doubt he deceived himself a good deal in his youth, but certainly his self-deception was not in the interests of vulgarity, for aristocracy meant to him a kind of disciplined distinction of personal existence which, presumably, he was so humble as not to expect from his art. What was involved in that notion of distinction can be learned from the use which Fitzgerald makes of the word "aristocracy" in one of those serious moments which occur in his most, frivolous Saturday Evening Post stories; he says of the life of the young man of the story, who during the war was on duty behind the lines, that "it was not so bad—except that when the infantry came limping back from the trenches he wanted to be one of them. The sweat and mud they wore seemed only one of those ineffable symbols of aristocracy that were forever eluding him." Fitzgerald was perhaps the last notable writer to affirm the Romantic fantasy, descended from the Renaissance, of personal ambition and heroism, of life committed to, or thrown away for, some ideal of self. To us it will no doubt come more and more to seem a merely boyish dream; the nature of our society requires the young man to find his distinction through cooperation, subordination, and an expressed piety of social usefulness, and although a few young men have made Fitzgerald into a hero of art, it is likely that even to these admirers the whole nature of his personal fantasy is not comprehensible, for young men find it harder and harder to understand the youthful heroes of Balzac and Stendhal, they increasingly find reason to blame the boy whose generosity is bound up with his will and finds its expression in a large, strict, personal demand upon life.

I am aware that I have involved Fitzgerald with a great many great names and that it might be felt by some that this can do him no service, the disproportion being so large. But the disproportion will seem large only to those who think of Fitzgerald chiefly through his early public legend of heedlessness. Those who have a clear recollection of the mature work or who have read *The Crack-Up* will at least not think of the disproportion as one of kind. Fitzgerald himself did not, and it is by a man's estimate of himself that we must begin to estimate him. For all the engaging self-depreciation which was part of his peculiarly American charm, he put himself, in all modesty, in the line of greatness, he judged himself in a large way. When he writes of his depression, of his "dark night of the soul" where "it is always three o'clock in the morning," he not only derives the phrase from St. John of the Cross but adduces the analogous black despairs of Wordsworth, Keats, and Shelley. A novel with Ernest Hemingway as the model of its hero suggests to him Stendhal portraying the Byronic man, and he defends *The Great Gatsby* from some critical remark of Edmund Wilson's by comparing it with *The Brothers Karamazov*. Or again, here is the stuff of his intellectual pride at the very moment that he speaks of giving it up, as years before he had given up the undergraduate fantasies of valor: "The old dream of being an entire man in the Goethe-Byron-Shaw tradition . . . has been relegated to the junk heap of the shoulder pads worn for one day on the Princeton freshman football field and the overseas cap never worn overseas." And was it, that old dream, unjustified? To take but one great name, the one that on first thought seems the least relevant of all—between Goethe at twenty-four the author of *Werther*, and Fitzgerald, at twenty-four the author of *This Side of Paradise*, there is not really so entire a difference as piety and textbooks might make us think; both the young men so handsome, both winning immediate and notorious success, both rather more interested in life than in art, each the spokesman and symbol of his own restless generation.

It is hard to overestimate the benefit which came to Fitzgerald from his having consciously placed himself in the line of the great. He was a "natural," but he did not have the contemporary American novelist's belief that if he compares himself with the past masters, or if he takes thought—which, for a writer, means really knowing what his predecessors have done—he will endanger the integrity of his natural gifts. To read Fitzgerald's letters to his daughter—they are among the best and most affecting letters I know—and to catch the tone in which he speaks about the literature of the past, or to read the notebooks he faithfully kept, indexing them as Samuel Butler had done, and to perceive how continuously he thought about literature, is to have some clue to the secret of the continuing power of Fitzgerald's work.

The Great Gatsby, for example, after a quarter-century is still as fresh as when it first appeared; it has even gained in weight and relevance, which can be said of very few American books of its time. This, I think, is to be attributed to the specifically intellectual courage with which it was conceived and executed, a courage which implies Fitzgerald's grasp—both in the sense of awareness and of appropriation—of the traditional resources available to him. Thus, *The Great Gatsby* has its interest as a record of contemporary manners, but this might only have served to date it, did not Fitzgerald take the given moment of history as something more than a mere circumstance, did he not, in the manner of the great French novelists of the nineteenth century, seize the given moment as a moral fact. The same boldness of intellectual grasp accounts for the success of the conception of its hero— Gatsby is said by some to be not quite credible, but the question of any literal credibility he may or may not have becomes trivial before the large significance he implies. For Gatsby, divided between power and dream, comes inevitably to stand for America itself. Ours is the only nation that prides itself upon a dream and gives its name to one, "the American dream." We are told that "the truth was that Jay Gatsby of West Egg, Long Island, sprang from his Platonic conception of himself. He was a son of God—a phrase which, if it means anything, means just that—and he must be about His Father's business, the service of a vast, vulgar, and meretricious beauty." Clearly it is Fitzgerald's intention that our mind should turn to the thought of the nation that has sprung from its "Platonic conception" of itself. To the world it is anomalous in America, just as in the novel it is anomalous in Gatsby, that so much raw power should be haunted by envisioned romance. Yet in that anomaly lies, for good or bad, much of the truth of our national life, as, at the present moment, we think about it.

Then, if the book grows in weight of significance with the years, we can be sure that this could not have happened had its form and style not been as right as they are. Its form is ingenious—with the ingenuity, however, not of craft but of intellectual intensity. The form, that is, is not the result of careful "plotting"—the form of a good novel never is—but is rather the result of the necessities of the story's informing idea, which require the sharpness of radical foreshortening. Thus, it will be observed, the characters are not "developed": the wealthy and brutal Tom Buchanan, haunted by his "scientific" vision of the doom of civilization, the vaguely guilty, vaguely homosexual Jordan Baker, the dim Wolfsheim, who fixed the World Series of 1919, are treated, we might say, as if they were ideographs, a method of economy that is reinforced by the ideographic use that is made of the Washington Heights flat, the terrible "valley of ashes" seen from the Long Island Railroad, Gatsby's incoherent parties, and the huge sordid eyes of the oculist's advertising sign. (It is a technique which gives the novel an affinity with *The Waste Land*, between whose author and Fitzgerald there existed a reciprocal admiration.) Gatsby himself, once stated, grows only in the understanding of the narrator. He is allowed to say very little in his own person. Indeed, apart from the famous "Her voice is full of money," he says only one memorable thing, but that remark is overwhelming in its intellectual audacity: when he is forced to admit that his lost Daisy did perhaps love her husband, he says, "In any case it was just personal." With that sentence he achieves an insane greatness, convincing us that he really is a Platonic conception of himself, really some sort of Son of God.

What underlies all success in poetry, what is even more important than the shape of the poem or its wit of metaphor, is the poet's voice. It either gives us confidence in what is being said or it tells us that we do not need to listen; and it carries both the modulation and the living form of what is being said. In the novel no less than in the poem, the voice of the author is the decisive factor. We are less consciously aware of it in the novel, and, in speaking of the elements of a novel's art, it cannot properly be exemplified by quotation because it is continuous and cumulative. In Fitzgerald's work the voice of his prose is of the essence of his success. We hear in it at once the tenderness toward human desire that modifies a true firmness of moral judgment. It is, I would venture to say, the normal or ideal voice of the novelist. It is characteristically modest, yet it has in it, without apology or self-consciousness, a largeness, even a stateliness, which derives from Fitzgerald's connection with tradition and with mind, from his sense of what has been done before and the demands which this past accomplishment makes. ". . . I became aware of the old island here that flowered once for Dutch sailors' eyes—a fresh green breast of the new world. Its vanished trees, the trees that had made way for Gatsby's house, had once pandered in whispers to the last and greatest of all human dreams; for a transitory and enchanted moment man must have held his breath in the presence of this continent, compelled into an aesthetic contemplation he neither understood nor desired, face to face for the last time in history with something commensurate to his capacity for wonder." Here, in the well-known passage, the voice is a little dramatic, a little *intentional*, which is not improper to a passage in climax and conclusion, but it will the better suggest in brief compass the habitual music of Fitzgerald's seriousness.

Fitzgerald lacked prudence, as his heroes did, lacked that blind instinct of self-protection which the writer needs and the American writer needs in double measure. But that is all he lacked—and it is the generous fault, even the heroic fault. He said of his Gatsby, "If personality is an unbroken series of successful gestures, there was something gorgeous about him, some heightened sensitivity to the promises of life, as if he were related to one of those intricate machines that register earthquakes ten thousand miles away. This responsiveness had nothing to do with that flabby impressionability which is dignified under the name of 'the creative temperament'—it was an extraordinary gift for hope, a romantic readiness such as I have never found in any other person and which it is not likely I shall ever find again." And it is so that we are drawn to see Fitzgerald himself as he stands in his exemplary role.

MALCOLM COWLEY

The Romance of Money

1

Those who were lucky enough to be born a little before the end of the last century, in any of the years from 1895 to 1900, went through much of their lives with a feeling that the new century was about to be placed in their charge; it was like a business in financial straits that could be rescued by a timely change in management. As Americans and optimists, they believed that the business was fundamentally sound. They identified themselves with the century; its teens were their teens, troubled but confident; its World War, not yet known as the First, was theirs to fight on the winning side; its reckless twenties were their twenties. As they launched into their careers, they looked about for spokesmen, and the first one they found—though soon they would have doubts about him—was F. Scott Fitzgerald.

Among his qualifications for the role was the sort of background that his generation regarded as typical. Scott was a Midwestern boy, born in St. Paul on September 24, 1896, to a family of Irish descent that had some social standing and a very small fortune inherited by the mother. The fortune kept diminishing year by year, and the Fitzgeralds, like all families in their situation, had to think a lot about money. When the only son was eleven they were living in Buffalo, where the father was working for Procter and Gamble. "One afternoon," Fitzgerald told a reporter thirty years later, ". . .

the phone rang and my mother answered it. I didn't understand what she said, but I felt that disaster had come to us. My mother, a little while before, had given me a quarter to go swimming. I gave the money back to her. I knew something terrible had happened and I thought she couldn't spare the money now. 'Dear God,' I prayed, 'please don't let us go to the poorhouse.'

"A little later my father came home. I had been right. He had lost his job." More than that, as Fitzgerald said, "He had lost his essential drive, his immaculateness of purpose." The family moved back to St. Paul, where the father worked as a wholesale grocery salesman, earning hardly enough to pay for his desk space. It was help from a pious aunt that enabled Scott to fulfill his early ambition of going to an Eastern preparatory school, then going to Princeton.

In 1917 practically the whole student body went off to war. Fitzgerald went off in style, having received a provisional commission as second lieutenant in the regular army. Before leaving Princeton in November, he ordered his uniform at Brooks Brothers and gave the manuscript of a first novel to his faculty mentor, Christian Gauss, not yet dean of the college, but a most persuasive teacher of European literature. Gauss, honest as always, told him that it wasn't good enough to publish. Not at all discouraged, Fitzgerald reworked it completely, writing twelve hours a day during his weekends at training camp and his first furlough. When the second draft was finished, he sent it to Shane Leslie, the Irish man of letters, who had shown some interest in his work. Leslie spent ten days correcting and punctuating the script, then sent it to Scribners, his own publishers. "Really if Scribner takes it," Fitzgerald said in a letter to Edmund Wilson, "I know I'll wake some morning and find that the debutantes have made me famous overnight. I really believe that no one else could have written so searchingly the story of the youth of our generation."

Scribners sent back the novel, rightly called *The Romantic Egotist*, while expressing some regret, and Maxwell Perkins, who was still too young to be the senior editor, suggested revisions that might make it acceptable. Fitzgerald tried to follow the suggestions and resubmitted the manuscript that summer. In August it was definitely rejected, and Fitzgerald then asked Perkins as a favor to submit it to two other publishers, one radical and one conservative. His letter was dated from Camp Sheridan, in Alabama, where he was soon to be named aide-de-camp to Major General J. A. Ryan. It was at a dance in Montgomery that he fell in love with a judge's daughter, Zelda Sayre, whom he described to his friends as "the most beautiful girl in Alabama *and* Georgia"; one state wasn't big enough to encompass his admiration. "I didn't have the two top things: great animal magnetism or money," he wrote years afterward in his notebook. "I had the two second things, though: good looks and intelligence. So I always got the top girl."

He was engaged to the judge's daughter, but they couldn't marry until he was able to support her. After being discharged from the army—without getting overseas, as I noted—he went to New York and looked for a job. Neither the radical nor the conservative publisher had shown interest in his novel. All his stories were coming back from the magazines, and at one time he had 122 rejection slips pinned in a frieze around his cheap bedroom on Morningside Heights. The job he found was with an advertising agency and his pay started at $90 a month, with not much chance of rapid advancement; the only praise he received was for a slogan written for a steam laundry in Muscatine, Iowa: "We keep you clean in Muscatine." He was trying to save money, but the girl in Alabama saw that the effort was hopeless and broke off the engagement on the score of common sense. Fitzgerald borrowed from his classmates, stayed drunk for three weeks, and then went home to St. Paul to write the novel once again, this time with another ending and a new title, *This Side of Paradise*. Scribners accepted it on that third submission. The book was so different from other novels of the time, Max Perkins wrote him, "that it is hard to prophesy how it will sell, but we are all for taking a chance and supporting it with vigor."

This Side of Paradise, published at the end of March 1920, is a very young man's novel and memory book. The author put into it samples of everything he had written until that time—short stories, essays, poems, prose poems, sketches, and dialogues—and he also put himself into it, after taking a promotion in social rank. The hero, Amory Blaine, instead of being a poor relative has been reared as the heir of millions, but he looks and talks like Fitzgerald, besides reading the same books (listed in one passage after another) and falling in love with the same girls. The story told in the novel, with many digressions, is how Amory struggles for self-knowledge and for less provincial standards than those of the Princeton eating clubs. "I know myself," he says at the end, "but that is all." Fitzgerald passed a final judgment on the novel in 1938, when he said in a letter to Max Perkins, "I think it is now one of the funniest books since *Dorian Gray* in its utter spuriousness—and then, here and there, I find a page that is very real and living."

Some of the living pages are the ones that recount the eating-club elections, the quarrel between Amory and his first flame, Isabelle—Fitzgerald would always be good on quarrels—the courting of Rosalind Connage, and Amory's three-weeks drunk when Rosalind throws him over. Besides having a spurious and imitative side, the novel proved that Fitzgerald had started with gifts of his own, which included an easy narrative style rich with images, a sense of comedy, and a natural ear for dialogue. Its memorable feature, however, was that it announced a change in standards. "Here was a new generation," Fitzgerald or his hero, it isn't clear which, says in the last chapter, "shouting the old cries, learning the old creeds, through a revery of long days and nights; destined finally to go out into that dirty gray turmoil to follow love and pride; a new generation dedicated more than the last to the fear of poverty and the worship of success; grown up to find all gods dead, all wars fought, all faiths in man shaken." With energy, candor, and a sort of innocence, Fitzgerald (or the hero) was speaking for his contemporaries. They recognized the voice as their own, and his elders listened.

Suddenly the magazines were eager to print Fitzgerald's stories and willing to pay high prices for them. The result shows in his big ledger: in 1919 he earned $879 by his writing; in 1920 he earned $18,850—and managed to end the year in debt.[1] Early success and princely spending had been added to everything else that made him stand out as a representative of his generation; and Fitzgerald was beginning to believe in his representative quality. He was learning that when he wrote truly about his dreams and misadventures and discoveries, other people recognized themselves in the picture.

The point has to be made that Fitzgerald wasn't "typical" of his own period or any other. He lived harder than most people have ever lived and acted out his dreams with an extraordinary intensity of emotion. The dreams themselves were not at all unusual: in the beginning they were dreams of becoming a football star and a big man in college, of being a hero on the battlefield, of winning through to financial success, and of getting the top girl. They were the commonplace visions shared by almost all the young men of his age and background, especially by those who were forging ahead in the business world; in many ways Fitzgerald was closer to them than he was to the other serious writers of his generation. It was the emotion he put into his dreams, and the honesty with which he expressed the emotion, that made them seem distinguished. By feeling intensely he made his readers believe in the unique value of the world in which they lived. He was to say later, writing in the third person, that he continued to feel grateful to the Jazz Age because "It bore him up, flattered him and gave him more money than he had dreamed of, simply for telling people that he felt as they did."

At the beginning of April 1920, Zelda came to New York and they were married in the rectory of St. Patrick's Cathedral—although Zelda's family was Episcopalian and Scott had ceased to be a good Catholic. They set up housekeeping at the Biltmore. To their bewilderment they found themselves adopted not as a Midwesterner and a Southerner respectively, not even as detached observers, but—Scott afterward wrote—"as the arch type of what New York wanted." A new age was beginning, and Scott and Zelda were venturing into it innocently, hand in hand. Zelda said, "It was always tea-time or late at night." Scott said, "We felt like children in a great bright unexplored barn."

2

Scott also said, "America was going on the greatest, gaudiest spree in history and there was going to be plenty to tell about it." There is still plenty to tell about it, in the light of a new age that continues to be curious about the 1920s and usually misjudges them. The gaudiest spree in history was also a moral revolt, and beneath the revolt were social transformations. The 1920s were the age when puritanism was under attack, with the Protestant churches losing their dominant position. They were the age when the country ceased to be English and Scottish and when the children of later immigrations moved forward to take their places in the national life. Theodore Dreiser, whom Fitzgerald regarded as the greatest living American writer, was South German Catholic by descent, H. L. Mencken, the most influential critic, was North German Protestant, and Fitzgerald did not forget for a moment that one side of his own family was "straight potato-famine Irish." Most of his heroes have Irish names and all except Gatsby are city-bred, thus reflecting another social change. The 1920s were the age when American culture became urban instead of rural and when New York set the social and intellectual standards of the country, while its own standards were being set by transplanted Southerners and Midwesterners like Zelda and Scott.

More essentially the 1920s were the age when a production ethic—of saving and self-denial in order to accumulate capital for new enterprises—gave way to a consumption ethic that was needed to provide markets for the new commodities that streamed from the production lines. Instead of being exhorted to save money, more and more of it, people were being exhorted in a thousand ways to buy, enjoy, use once and throw away, in order to buy a later and more expensive model. They followed the instructions, with the result that more goods were produced and consumed or wasted and money was easier to earn or borrow than ever in the past. Foresight went out of fashion. "The Jazz Age," Fitzgerald was to say, "now raced along under its own power, served by great filling stations full of money. . . . Even when you were broke you didn't worry about money, because it was in such profusion around you."

Young men and women in the 1920s had a sense of reckless confidence not only about money but about life in general. It was part of their background: they had grown up in the years when middle-class Americans read Herbert Spencer and believed in the doctrine of automatic social evolution. The early twentieth century seemed to confirm the doctrine. Things were getting better each year: more grain was reaped, more iron was smelted, more rails were laid, more profits earned, more records broken, as new cities were founded and all cities grew, as the country grew, as the world apparently grew in wealth and wisdom toward the goal of universal peace— and those magical results were obtained, so it seemed, by each man's seeking his private interest. After 1914 the notion of automatic progress lost most of its support in events, but retained its place in the public mind. Young men and women of Fitzgerald's time, no matter how rebellious and cynical they thought of themselves as being, still clung to their childhood notion that the world would improve without their help; that was one of the reasons why most of them felt excused from seeking the common good. Plunging into their personal adventures, they took risks that didn't impress them as being risks because, in their hearts, they believed in the happy ending.

They were truly rebellious, however, and were determined to make an absolute break with the standards of the prewar generation. The distinction between highbrow and lowbrow (or liberal and conservative) was not yet sharp enough to divide American society; the gulf was between the young and the old. The younger set paid few visits to their parents' homes and some of them hardly exchanged a social word with men or women over forty. The elders were straitlaced or stuffy, and besides they had made a mess of the world; they were discredited in younger eyes not only by the war and what followed it—especially Prohibition—but also, after 1923, by the scandals that clustered round Teapot Dome and the little green house on K Street, in Washington, where members of President Harding's Cabinet, and sometimes the President himself, played their cozy games of poker with the oil barons. So let the discredited elders keep to themselves; the youngsters would then have a free field in which to test their standards of the good life.

Those standards were elementary and close to being savage. Rejecting almost everything else, the spokesmen for the new generation celebrated the value of simple experiences such as love, foreign travel, good food, and drunkenness. "Immortal drunkenness!" Thomas Wolfe was to exclaim in a novel,[2] interrupting the adventures of his hero. "What tribute can we ever pay, what song can we ever sing, what swelling praise can ever be sufficient to express the joy, the gratefulness and love which we, who have known youth and hunger in America, have owed to alcohol? . . . You came to us with music, poetry, and wild joy when we were twenty, when we reeled home at night through the old moon-whitened streets of Boston and heard our friend, our comrade and our dead companion, shout through the silence of the moonwhite square: 'You are a poet and the world is yours.'" Others besides Wolfe heard the voice repeating "You are a poet!" and they hastened to enjoy their birthday-present world by loving, traveling, eating, drinking, dancing all night, and writing truthfully about their mornings after. They all recognized the value of being truthful, even if it hurt their families or their friends and most of all if it hurt themselves; almost any action seemed excusable and even admirable in those days if one simply told the truth about it, without boasting, without shame.

They liked to say yes to every proposal that suggested excitement. Will you take a new job, throw up the job, go to Paris and starve, travel round the world in a freighter? Will you get married, leave your husband, spend a weekend for two in Biarritz? Will you ride through Manhattan on the roof of a taxi and then go bathing in the Plaza fountain? "W Y B M A D I I T Y?" read a sign on the mirror behind the bar of a popular speakeasy, the Dizzy Club. Late at night you asked the bartender what it meant, and he answered, "Will You Buy Me A Drink If I Tell You?" The answer was yes, always yes, and the fictional heroine of the 1920s was Serena Blandish, the girl who couldn't say no. Or the heroine was Joyce's Molly Bloom as she dreamed about the days when she was being courted: ". . . and I thought as well him as another and then I asked him with my eyes to ask again yes and then he asked me would I yes to say yes my mountain flower and first I put my arms around him yes and drew him down to me so he could feel my breasts all perfume yes and his heart was going like mad and yes I said yes I will Yes."

The masculine ideal of the 1920s was what Fitzgerald called "the old dream of being an entire man in the Goethe-Byron-Shaw tradition, with an opulent American touch, a sort of combination of J. P. Morgan, Topham Beauclerk and St. Francis of Assisi." The entire man would be one who "did everything," good and bad, who realized all the potentialities of his nature and thereby acquired wisdom. The entire man, in the 1920s, was one who followed the Rule of the Thelemites as revealed by Rabelais: Fais ce que vouldras, "Do what you will!" But that rule implied a second imperative like an echo: "Will!" To be admired by the 1920s young men had to will all sorts of actions and had to possess enough energy and boldness to carry out even momentary wishes. They lived in the moment with what they liked to call "an utter disregard of consequences." In spirit they all made pilgrimages to the abbey of the Thelemites, where they consulted the Oracle of the Divine Bottle and received for answer the one word Trinc. They obeyed the oracle and drank, in those days of the Volstead Act when drinking was a rite of comradeship and an act of rebellion. As Fitzgerald said at the time, they drank "cocktails before meals like Americans, wines and brandies like Frenchmen, beer like Germans, whiskey-and-soda like the English . . . this preposterous mélange that was like a gigantic cocktail in a nightmare."

But the 1920s were not so much a drinking as a dancing age—the Jazz Age, in the phrase that Fitzgerald made his own. In those days one heard jazz everywhere—from orchestras in ballrooms, from wind-up phonographs in the parlor, from loudspeakers blaring in variety stores, lunch wagons, even machine shops—and jazz wasn't regarded as something to listen to and be cool about, without even tapping one's feet; jazz was music with a purpose, *Gebrauchsmusik*; it was music to which you danced:

> *I met her in Chicago and she was married.*
>   *Dance all day,*
> *leave your man, Sweet Mamma, and come away;*
> *manicured smiles and kisses, to dance all day, all day.*
>   *How it was sad.*
>
> *Please, Mr. Orchestra, play us another tune.*
>
> My daddy went and left me and left the cupboard bare.
> Who will pay the butcher bill now Daddy isn't there?
>   *Shuffle your feet.*
> Found another daddy and he taught me not to care,
>   and how to care.
> Found another daddy that I'll follow anywhere.
>   *Shuffle your feet, dance,*
>
> *dance among the tables, dance across the floor,*
> *slip your arm around me, we'll go dancing out the door,*
> *Sweet Mamma, anywhere, through any door.*
> *Wherever the banjos play is Tennessee.*

Jazz carried with it a constant message of change, excitement, violent escape, with an undertone of sadness, but with a promise of enjoyment somewhere around the corner of next week, perhaps at midnight in a distant country. The young men heard the message and followed it anywhere, through any door, even the one that led into what was then, for Americans, the new world of difficult art. They danced too much, they drank too much, but they also worked, with something of the same desperation; they worked to rise, to earn social rank, to sell, to advertise, to organize, to invent gadgets, and to create enduring works of literature. In ten years, before losing their first vitality, they gave a new tempo to American life.

Fitzgerald not only represented the age but came to suspect that he had helped to create it, by setting forth a pattern of conduct that would be followed by persons a little younger than himself. That it was a dangerous pattern was something he recognized almost from the beginning. "If I had anything to do with creating the manners of the contemporary American girl I certainly made a botch of the job," he said in a 1925 letter. In a notebook he observed that one of his relatives was still a flapper in the 1930s. "There is no doubt," he added, "that she originally patterned herself upon certain immature and unfortunate writings of mine, so that I have a special fondness for—as for one who has lost an arm or a leg in one's service." When he was living at La Paix, a brown wooden late-Victorian lodge on a thirty-acre estate near Baltimore, a drunken young man teetered up to his door and said, "I had to see you. I feel I owe you more than I can say. I feel that you formed my life." It was not the young man—later a widely read novelist and an alcoholic–but Fitzgerald himself who became the principal victim of his capacity for creating fictional types in life. "Sometimes," he told another visitor to La Paix, late at night, "I don't know whether Zelda and I are real or whether we are characters in one of my novels."

That was in the spring of 1933, a few weeks after the banks had closed all over the country. It seemed then that the whole generation of the 1920s had been defeated by life, and yet, in their own defeat, Scott and Zelda were still its representative figures.

3

Fitzgerald never lost a quality that very few writers are able to acquire: a sense of living in history. Manners and morals were changing all through his life and he set himself the task of recording the changes. These were revealed to him, not by statistics or news reports, but in terms of living characters, and the characters were revealed by gestures, each appropriate to a certain year. He wrote: "One day in 1926 we"—meaning the members of his generation— "looked down and found we had flabby arms and a fat pot and we couldn't say boop-boop-a-doop to a Sicilian. . . . By 1927 a widespread neurosis began to be evident, faintly signaled, like a nervous beating of the feet, by the popularity of cross-word puzzles. . . . By this time"—also in 1927— "contemporaries of mine had begun to disappear into the dark maw of violence. . . . By 1928 Paris had grown suffocating. With each new shipment of Americans spewed up by the boom the quality fell off, until towards the end there was something sinister about the crazy boatloads."

He tried to find the visible act that revealed the moral quality inherent in a certain moment of time. He was haunted by time, as if he wrote in a room full of clocks and calendars. He made lists by the hundred, including lists of the popular songs, the football players, the top debutantes (with the types of beauty they cultivated), the hobbies, and the slang expressions of a given year; he felt that all those names and phrases belonged to the year and helped to reveal its momentary color. "After all," he said in an otherwise undistinguished magazine story, "any given moment has its value; it can be questioned in the light of after-events, but the moment remains. The young prince in velvet gathered in lovely domesticity around the queen amid the hush of rich draperies may presently grow up to be Pedro the Cruel or Charles the Mad, but the moment of beauty was there."

Fitzgerald lived in his great moments, and lived in them again when he reproduced their drama, but he also stood apart from them and coldly reckoned their causes and consequences. That is his doubleness or irony, and it is one of his distinguishing marks as a writer. He took part in the ritual orgies of his time, but he kept a secretly detached position, regarding himself as a pauper living among millionaires, a Celt among Sassenachs, and a sullen peasant among the nobility; he said that his point of vantage "was the dividing line between two generations," prewar and postwar. Always he cultivated a double vision. In his novels and stories he was trying to intensify the glitter of life in the Princeton eating clubs, on the north shore of Long Island, in Hollywood, and on the Riviera; he surrounded his characters with a mist of admiration, and at the same time he kept driving the mist away. He liked to know "where the milk is watered and the sugar sanded, the rhinestone passed for the diamond and the stucco for stone." It was as if all his fiction described a big dance to which he had taken, as he once wrote, the prettiest girl:

> *There was an orchestra–Bingo-Bango*
> *Playing for us to dance the tango*
> *And the people all clapped as we arose*
> *For her sweet face and my new clothes—*

and as if he stood at the same time outside the ballroom, a little Midwestern boy with his nose to the glass, wondering how much the tickets cost and who paid for the music. But it was not a dance he was watching so much as it was a drama of conflicting manners and aspirations in which he was both the audience and the leading actor. As audience he kept a cold eye on the actor's performance. He wrote of himself when he was twenty, "I knew that at bottom I lacked the essentials. At the last crisis, I knew that I had no real courage, perseverance or self-respect." Sixteen years later he was just as critical, and he said to a visitor at La Paix, "I've got a very limited talent. I'm a workman of letters, a professional. I know when to write and when to stop writing." It was the maximum of critical detachment, but it was combined with the maximum of immersion in the drama. He said in his notebook, and without the least exaggeration, "Taking things hard, from Ginevra to Joe Mankiewicz," mentioning the names of his first unhappy love and of the Hollywood producer who, so he thought, had ruined one of his best scripts: "That's the stamp that goes into my books so that people read it blind like Braille."

The drama he watched and in which he overplayed a leading part was a moral drama leading to rewards and punishments. "Sometimes I wish I had gone along with that gang," he said in a letter that discussed musical comedies and mentioned Cole Porter and Rodgers and Hart; "but I guess I am too much a moralist at heart and want to preach at people in some acceptable form, rather than to entertain them." The morality he wanted to preach was a simple one, in the midst of the prevailing confusion. Its four cardinal virtues were Industry, Discipline, Responsibility (in the sense of meeting one's social and financial obligations), and Maturity (in the sense of learning to expect little from life while continuing to make one's best efforts). Thus, his stories had a way of becoming fables. For virtues they displayed or failed to display, the characters were rewarded or punished in the end.

The handle by which he took hold of the characters was their dreams. These, as I said, might be commonplace or even cheap, but usually Fitzgerald managed to surround them with an atmosphere of the mysterious and illimitable or of the pitifully doomed. His great scenes were, so to speak, played to music: sometimes the music from a distant ballroom, sometimes that of a phonograph braying out a German tango, sometimes the wind in the leaves, sometimes the stark music of the heart. When there was no music, at least there were pounding rhythms: "The city's quick metropolitan rhythm of love and birth and death that supplied dreams to the unimaginative"; "The rhythm of the week-end, with its birth, its planned gaieties and its announced end"; "New York's flashing, dynamic good looks, its tall man's quick-step." Fitzgerald's dream of his mature years, after he had outgrown the notion of becoming a big man in college, was also set to music, perhaps to the *Unfinished Symphony*; it was the dream of becoming a great writer, specifically a great novelist who would do for American society in his time what Turgenev, for example, had done for the old regime in Russia.

It was not his dream to be a poet, yet that was how he started and in some ways he remained a poet primarily. He noted, "The talent that matures early is usually of the poetic type, which mine was in large part." His favorite author was Keats, not Turgenev or Flaubert. "I suppose I've read it a hundred times," he said of the "Ode on a Grecian Urn." "About the tenth time I began to know what it was about, and caught the chime in it and the exquisite inner mechanics. Likewise with the 'Nightingale,' which I can never read without tears in my eyes; likewise 'The Pot of Basil,' with its great stanzas about the two brothers. . . . Knowing these things very young and granted an ear, one could scarcely ever afterwards be unable to distinguish between gold and dross in what one read." When his daughter was learning to be a writer he advised her to read Keats and Browning and try her hand at a sonnet. He added, "The only thing that will help you is poetry, which is the most concentrated form of style."

Fitzgerald himself was a poet who never learned some of the elementary rules for writing prose. His grammar was shaky and his spelling definitely bad: for example, he wrote "ect." more often than "etc." and misspelled the name of his friend Monsignor Fay on the dedication page of *This Side of Paradise*. In his letters he always misspelled the given names of his first and last loves. He was not a student, for all the books he read; not a theoretician and perhaps one should flatly say, not a thinker. He counted on his friends to do much of his thinking for him; at Princeton it was John Peale Bishop who, he said, "made me see, in the course of a couple of months, the difference between poetry and non-poetry." Twenty years later, at the time of his crack-up, he re-examined his scale of values and found thinking incredibly difficult; he compared it to "the moving about of great secret trunks." He was then forced to the conclusion "That I had done very little thinking, save within the problems of my craft. For twenty years a certain man had been my intellectual conscience. That man was Edmund Wilson." Another contemporary "had been an artistic conscience to me. I had not imitated his infectious style, because my own style, such as it is, was formed before he published anything, but there was an awful pull towards him when I was on the spot."

Fitzgerald was making the confession in order to keep straight with himself, not to forestall any revelation that might have been made by his critics. The critics would have said that there was little of Wilson's influence perceptible in his work and still less of Hemingway's, although he once wrote a story about two dogs, "Shaggy's Morning," that is a delicate and deliberate pastiche of the Hemingway manner. By listening hard one can overhear a few, a very few suggestions of Hemingway in the dialogue of other stories, especially the later ones, but Fitzgerald was faithful to his own vision of the world and his way of expressing it. His debt to Wilson and Hemingway is real, but hard to define. In essence they were two older-brother figures (though Hemingway was younger than Fitzgerald); two different models of literary conduct. Though his style of life bore no resemblance to either of theirs, he used them to test and define his moral attitude toward the problems of his craft.

4

There was one respect in which Fitzgerald, much as he regarded himself as a representative figure of the age, was completely different from most of its serious writers. In that respect he was, as I said, much closer to the men of his college year who were trying to get ahead in the business world; like them he was fascinated by the process of earning and spending money. The young businessmen of his time, much more than those of a later generation, had been taught to measure success, failure, and even virtue in pecuniary terms. They had learned in school and Sunday school that virtue was rewarded with money and vice punished by the loss of money; apparently their one aim should be to earn lots of it fast. Yet money was only a convenient and inadequate symbol for what they dreamed of earning. The best of them were like Jay Gatsby in having "some heightened sensitivity to the promise of life"; or they were like another Fitzgerald hero, Dexter Green of "Winter Dreams," who "wanted not association with glittering things and glittering people—he wanted the glittering things themselves." Their real dream was that of achieving a new status and a new essence, of rising to a loftier place in the mysterious hierarchy of human worth.

The serious writers also dreamed of rising to a loftier status, but—except for Fitzgerald—they felt that moneymaking was the wrong way to rise. They liked money if it reached them in the form of gifts or legacies or publishers' advances; they would have liked it in the form of prizes or fellowships, though there were few of these to be had in the 1920s; but they were afraid of high earned incomes because of what the incomes stood for: obligations, respectability, time lost from their essential work, expensive habits that would drive them to seek still higher incomes—in short, a series of involvements in the commercial culture that was hostile to art. "If you want to ruin a writer," I used to hear some of them saying, "just give him a big magazine contract or a job at ten thousand a year." Many of them tried to preserve their independence by earning only enough to keep them alive while writing; a few regarded themselves as heroes of poverty and failure. "Now I can write," Faulkner said when his third novel was turned down and he thought he would never be published again.

A disdainful attitude toward money went into the texture of Faulkner's work, as into that of many others. The work was non-commercial in the sense of being written in various new styles that the public was slow to accept. It was an age of literary experiment when young writers were moving in all directions simultaneously. They were showing the same spirit of adventure and exploration in fiction that their contemporaries were showing in the business world. That spirit made them part of the age, but at the same time they were trying to stand apart from it, and some of them looked back longingly to other ages when, so they liked to think, artists had wealthy patrons and hence were able to live outside the economic system.

Fitzgerald immersed himself in the age and always remained close to the business world which they were trying to evade. That world was the background of his stories, and these performed a business function in themselves, by supplying the narrative that readers followed like a thread through the labyrinth of advertising in the slick-paper magazines. He did not divorce himself from readers by writing experimental prose or refusing to tell a story. His very real originality was a matter of mood and subject and image rather than of structure, and it was more evident in his novels than in his stories, good as the stories often were. Although he despised the trade of writing for magazines—or despised it with part of his mind—he worked at it honestly. It yielded him a large income that he couldn't have earned in any other fashion, and the income was necessary to his self-respect.

Fitzgerald kept an accurate record of his earnings—in the big ledger in which he also kept a record of his deeds and misdeeds, as if to strike a bookkeeper's balance between them—but he was vague about his expenditures and usually vague about his possessions, including his balance in the bank. Once he asked a cashier, "How much money have I got?" The cashier looked in a big book and answered without even scowling, "None." Fitzgerald resolved to be more thrifty, knowing he would break the resolution. "All big men have spent money freely," he explained in a letter to his mother. "I hate avarice or even caution." He had little interest in the physical objects that money could buy. On the other hand, he had a great interest in earning money, lots of it fast, because that was a gold medal offered with the blue ribbon for competitive achievement. Once the money was earned, he and Zelda liked to spend lots of it fast, usually for impermanent things: not for real estate, fine motorcars, or furniture, but for traveling expenses, the rent of furnished houses, the wages of nurses and servants; for parties, party dresses, and feather fans of five colors. Zelda was as proudly careless about money as an eighteenth-century nobleman's heir. Scott was more practical and had his penny-pinching moments, as if in memory of his childhood, but at other times he liked to spend without counting in order to enjoy a proud sense of potency.

In his attitude toward money he revealed the new spirit of an age when conspicuous accumulation was giving way to conspicuous earning and spending. It was an age when gold was melted down and became fluid; when wealth was no longer measured in possessions—land, houses, livestock, machinery—but rather in dollars per year, as a stream is measured by its flow; when for the first time the expenses of government were being met by income taxes more than by property and excise taxes; and when the new tax structure was making it somewhat more difficult to accumulate a stable and lasting fortune. Such fortunes still existed at the hardly accessible peak of the social system, which young men dreamed of reaching like Alpinists, but the romantic figures of the age were not capitalists properly speaking. They were salaried executives and advertising men, they were promoters, salesmen, stock gamblers, or racketeers, and they were millionaires in a new sense—not men each of whom owned a million dollars' worth of property, but men who lived in rented apartments and had nothing but stock certificates and insurance policies (or nothing but credit and the right connections), while spending more than the income of the old millionaires.

The change went deep into the texture of American society and deep into the feelings of Americans as individuals. Fitzgerald is its most faithful recorder, not only in the stories that earned him a place in the new high-income class, but also in his personal confessions. He liked to describe his vitality and his talent in pecuniary terms. When both of them temporarily disappeared, in his crack-up of the years 1935–36, he pictured the event as a sort of financial bankruptcy. He wrote (but without my italics), "I began to realize that for two years my life had been a *drawing on resources* that I did not possess, that I had been *mortgaging myself* physically and spiritually up to the hilt." Again he wrote, "When a new sky cut off the sun last spring, I didn't at first relate it to what had happened fifteen or twenty years ago. Only gradually did a certain family resemblance come through—an over-extension of the flank, a burning of the candle at both ends; a call upon physical resources that I did not command, *like a man overdrawing at his bank.* . . . There were plenty of *counterfeit coins* around that I could pass off instead of these"—that is, in spite of the honest emotions he had lost—"and I knew where I could get them at *a nickel on the dollar.*"

"Where was the leak," Fitzgerald asked, "through which, unknown to myself, my enthusiasm and my vitality had been steadily and prematurely trickling away?" Vitality was something liquid and it was equated with money, which was also liquid. The attitude was different from that which prevailed before World War I, when people spoke of saving money as "piling up the rocks," instead of filling the reservoir, and when the millionaire in the funny papers was "Mr. Gotrocks." In Freud's great system, which is based on his observation of nineteenth-century types, money is something solid, gold or silver, and the bodily product it suggests is excrement. Thus, the pursuit of money for its own sake develops from anal eroticism, and Freud maintains that the miser is almost always a constipated man. I doubt whether recent analysts have observed how money is losing its old symbolic value and how, in the American subconscious, it tends to be identified with other bodily products such as urine ("I just pee'd it away"), blood, sperm, or milk.

Fitzgerald was more closely involved with contemporary values than most of the professional analysts. He uses the new imagery in much of his confessional writing, and it becomes especially clear in a free-verse poem, "Our April Letter," which he wrote during his crack-up. Three lines of the poem read:

> *I have asked a lot of my emotions—one hundred and twenty stories. The price was high, right up with Kipling, because there was one little drop of something— not blood, not a tear, not my seed, but me more intimately than these, in every story, it was the extra I had. Now it has gone and I am just like you now.*
>
> *Once the phial was full—here is the bottle it came in.*
>
> *Hold on, there's a drop left there. . . . No, it was just the way the light fell.*

Note that the something more intimate than blood or tears or sperm— though suggested by all of these—had a monetary value and was being sold to the magazines at a price right up with what Kipling had been paid. Note also that in its absence Fitzgerald was no longer able to write salable stories, so that he came to identify emotional with financial bankruptcy. In that black year 1936 he was earning very little money and owed more than forty thousand dollars, but he kept a careful record of his debts and later paid off most of them, by living in a modest fashion even during the months when he was earning a big salary in Hollywood. He never became solvent, but his financial obligations were not so pressing at the end of his life, and he was doing some of his best work.

In writing about the romance of money, as he did in most of his earlier novels and stories, he was dealing not only with an intimate truth but also with what seemed to him the central truth of his American age. "Americans," he liked to say, "should be born with fins and perhaps they were—perhaps money was a form of fin."

5

One of his remarks about himself has often puzzled his critics. "D. H. Lawrence's great attempt to synthesize animal and emotional—things he left out," Fitzgerald wrote in his notebook, then added the comment, "Essential pre-Marxian. Just as I am essentially Marxian." He was never Marxian in any sense of the word that Marxians of whatever school would be willing to accept. It is true that he finally read well into *Das Kapital* and was impressed by "the terrible chapter," as he called it, "on 'The Working Day'"; but it left in him no trace of Marx's belief in the mission of the proletariat.

His picture of proletarian life was of something alien to his own background, mysterious and even criminal. It seems to have been symbolized in some of his stories—notably in "Winter Dreams" and "A Short Trip Home"—by the riverfront strip in St. Paul that languished in the shadow of the big houses on Summit Avenue; he described the strip as a gridiron of mean streets where consumptive or pugilistic youths lounged in front of poolrooms, their skins turned livid by the neon lights. In *The Great Gatsby* he must have been thinking about the lower levels of American society when he described the valley of ashes between West Egg and New York—"A fantastic farm," he calls it, "where ashes grow like wheat into ridges and hills and grotesque gardens; where ashes take the forms of houses and chimneys and rising smoke and, finally, with a transcendent effort, of men who move dimly and always crumbling through the powdery air." One of his early titles for the novel was "Among Ash Heaps and Millionaires"—as if he were setting the two against each other while suggesting a vague affinity between them. Tom Buchanan, the brutalized millionaire, finds a mistress in the valley of ashes.

In Fitzgerald's stories there can be no real struggle between this dimly pictured ash-gray proletariat and the bourgeoisie. On the other hand, there can be a different struggle that the author must have regarded, for a time, as essentially Marxian. It is the struggle I have already suggested, between wealth as fluid income and wealth as an inherited and solid possession—or rather, since Fitzgerald is not an essayist but a storyteller, it is between a man and a woman as representatives of the new and the old moneyed classes.

We are not allowed to forget that they are representatives. The man comes from a family with little or no money, but he manages to attend an Eastern university—most often Yale, to set a distance between the hero and the Princeton author. He then sets out to earn a fortune equal to that of his wealthy classmates. Usually what he earns is not a fortune but an impressively large income, after he has risen to the top of his chosen profession—which may be engineering or architecture or advertising or the laundry business or bootlegging or real estate or even, in one story, frozen fish; the heroes are never novelists, although one of them is said to be a successful playwright. When the heroes are halfway to the top, they fall in love.

The woman—or rather the girl—in a Fitzgerald story is as alluring as the youngest princess in a fairy tale. "In children's books," he says when presenting one heroine, "forests are sometimes made out of all-day suckers, boulders out of peppermints and rivers out of gently flowing, rippling molasses taffy. Such . . . localities exist, and one day a girl, herself little more than a child, sat dejected in the middle of one. It was all hers, she owned it; she owned Candy Town." Another heroine "was a stalk of ripe corn, but bound not as cereals are but as a rare first edition, with all the binder's art. She was lovely and expensive and about nineteen." Of still another heroine Fitzgerald says when she first appears that "Her childish beauty was wistful and sad about being so rich and sixteen." Later, when her father loses his money, the hero pays her a visit in London. "All around her," Fitzgerald says, "he could feel the vast Mortmain fortune melting down, seeping back into the matrix whence it had come." The hero thinks she might marry him, now that she has fallen almost to his financial level; but he finds that the Mortmain (or dead-hand) fortune, even though lost, is still a barrier between them. Note that the man is not attracted by the fortune in itself. He is not seeking money so much as position at the peak of the social hierarchy, and the girl becomes the symbol of that position, the incarnation of its mysterious power. That is Daisy Buchanan's charm for the great Gatsby and the reason why he directs his whole life toward winning back her love.

"She's got an indiscreet voice," Nick Carraway says of her. "It's full of—" and he hesitates.

"Her voice is full of money," Gatsby says.

And Nick, the narrator, thinks to himself, "That was it. I'd never understood before. It was full of money—that was the inexhaustible charm that rose and fell in it, the cymbals' song of it. . . . High in a white palace the king's daughter, the golden girl."

In Fitzgerald's stories a love affair is like secret negotiations between the diplomats of two countries which are not at peace and not quite at war. For a moment they forget their hostility, find it transformed into mutual inspection, attraction, even passion (though the passion is not physical); but the hostility will survive even in marriage, if marriage is to be their future. I called the lovers diplomats, ambassadors, and that is another way of saying that they are representatives. When they meet it is as if they were leaning toward each other from separate high platforms—the man from a platform built up of his former poverty, his ambition, his competitive triumphs, his ability to earn and spend always more, more; the girl from another platform covered with cloth of gold and feather fans of many colors, but beneath them a sturdy pile of stock certificates testifying to the ownership of mines, forests, factories, villages—all of Candy Town.

She is ownership embodied, as can be seen in one of the best of Fitzgerald's early stories, "Winter Dreams." A rising young man named Dexter Green takes home the daughter of a millionaire for whom he used to be a caddy. She is Judy Jones, "a slender enameled doll in cloth of gold: gold in a band at her head, gold in two slipper points at her dress's hem." The rising young man stops his coupé "in front of the great white bulk of the Mortimer Jones house, somnolent, gorgeous, drenched with the splendor of the damp moonlight. Its solidity startled him. The strong walls, the steel of the girders, the breadth and beam and pomp of it were there only to bring out the contrast with the young beauty beside him. It was sturdy to accentuate her slightness—as if to show what a breeze could be generated by a butterfly's wing." In legends butterflies are symbols of the soul. The inference is clear that, holding Judy in his arms, Dexter Green is embracing the spirit of a great fortune.

Nicole Warren, the heroine of *Tender Is the Night*, embodies the spirit of an even greater fortune. Fitzgerald says of her, in a familiar passage:

> Nicole was the product of much ingenuity and toil. For her sake trains began their run at Chicago and traversed the round belly of the continent to California; chicle factories fumed and link belts grew link by link in factories; men mixed toothpaste in vats and drew mouthwash out of copper hogs-heads; girls canned tomatoes quickly in August or worked rudely at the Five-and-Tens on Christmas Eve; half-breed Indians toiled on Brazilian coffee plantations and dreamers were muscled out of patent rights in new tractors—these were some of the people who gave a tithe to Nicole, and as the whole system swayed and thundered onward it lent a feverish bloom to such processes of hers as wholesale buying [of luxuries], like the flush of a fireman's face holding his post before a spreading blaze.

Sometimes Fitzgerald's heroines are candid, even brutal, about class relations. "Let's start right," Judy Jones says to Dexter Green on the first evening they spend alone together. "Who are you?"

"I'm nobody," Dexter tells her, without adding that he had been her father's caddy. "My career is largely a matter of futures."

"Are you poor?"

"No," he says frankly, "I'm probably making more money than any man my age in the Northwest. I know that's an obnoxious remark, but you advised me to start right."

"There was a pause," Fitzgerald adds. "Then she smiled and the corners
of her mouth drooped and an almost imperceptible sway brought her closer
to him, looking up into his eyes." Money brings them together, but later they
are separated by something undefined—a mere whim of Judy's, it would
seem, though one comes to suspect that the whim was based on her feeling
that she should marry a man of her own caste. Dexter, as he goes East to earn
a still larger income, is filled with regret for "the country of illusions, of
youth, of the richness of life, where his winter dreams had flourished." It
seems likely that Judy Jones, like Josephine Perry in a series of later stories,
was a character suggested by a Chicago debutante with whom Fitzgerald was
desperately in love during his first years at Princeton; afterward she made a
more sensible marriage. As for the general attitude toward the rich that
began to be expressed in "Winter Dreams," it is perhaps connected with his
experience in 1919, when he was not earning enough to support a wife and
Zelda broke off their engagement. Later he said of the time:

> During a long summer of despair I wrote a novel instead of
> letters, so it came out all right; but it came out all right for a
> different person. The man with the jingle of money in his pocket
> who married the girl a year later would always cherish an abiding
> distrust, an animosity, toward the leisure class—not the
> conviction of a revolutionist but the smoldering hatred of a
> peasant.

His mixture of feelings toward the very rich, which included curiosity
and admiration as well as distrust, is revealed in his treatment of a basic
situation that reappears in many of his stories. Of course he presented other
situations that were not directly concerned with the relation between social
classes. He wrote about the problem of adjusting oneself to life, which he
thought was especially difficult for self-indulgent American women. He
wrote about the manners of flappers, slickers, and jelly beans. He wrote
engagingly about his own boyhood. He wrote about the patching-up of
broken marriages, about the contrast between Northern and Southern life,
about Americans going to pieces in Europe, about the self-tortures of gifted
alcoholics, and in much of his later work—as notably in *The Last Tycoon*—he
was expressing admiration for inspired technicians, such as brain surgeons
and movie directors. But a great number of his stories, especially the early
ones, start with the basic situation I have mentioned: a rising young man of
the middle classes in love with the daughter of a very rich family. (Sometimes
the family is Southern, in which case it needn't be so rich, since a high social
status could still exist in the South without great wealth.)

From that beginning the story may take any one of several turns. The hero may marry the girl, but only after she loses her fortune or (as in "Presumption" and "'The Sensible Thing'") he gains an income greater than hers. He may lose the girl (as in "Winter Dreams") and always remember her with longing for his early aspirations. In "The Bridal Party" he resigns himself to the loss after being forced to recognize the moral superiority of the rich man she has married. In "More Than Just a House" he learns that the girl is empty and selfish and ends by marrying her good sister; in "The Rubber Check" he marries Ellen Mortmain's quiet cousin. There is, however, still another development out of the Fitzgerald situation that comes closer to revealing his ambiguous feeling toward the very rich. To state it simply—too simply—the rising young man wins the rich girl and then is destroyed by her wealth or her relatives.

It is the ballad of young Lochinvar come out of the West, but with a tragic ending–as if fair Ellen's kinsmen, armed and vengeful, had overtaken the pair or as if Ellen herself had betrayed the hero. Fitzgerald used it for the first time in a fantasy, "The Diamond As Big As the Ritz," which he wrote in St. Paul during the winter of 1921–22. In the fashion of many fantasies, it reveals the author's cast of mind more clearly than his realistic stories. It deals with the adventures of a boy named John T. Unger (we might read "Hunger"), who was born in a town on the Mississippi called Hades, though it also might be called St. Paul. He is sent away to St. Midas', which is "the most expensive and most exclusive boys' preparatory school in the world," and there he meets Percy Washington, who invites him to spend the summer at his home in the West. On the train Percy confides to him that his father is the richest man alive and owns a diamond bigger than the Ritz-Carlton Hotel.

The description of the Washington mansion, in its hidden valley that wasn't even shown on maps of the U.S. Geodetic Survey, is fantasy mingled with burlesque, but then the familiar Fitzgerald note appears. John falls in love with Percy's younger sister, Kismine. After an idyllic summer Kismine tells him accidentally—she had meant to keep the secret—that he will very soon be murdered, like all the former guests of the Washingtons. "It was done very nicely," she explains to him. "They were drugged while they were asleep— and their families were always told that they died of scarlet fever in Butte. . . . I shall probably have visitors too—I'll harden up to it. We can't let such an inevitable thing as death stand in the way of enjoying life while we have it. Think how lonesome it would be out here if we never had *anyone*. Why, father and mother have sacrificed some of their best friends just as we have."

In *The Great Gatsby*, Tom and Daisy Buchanan would also sacrifice some of their best friends. "They were careless people, Tom and Daisy—they smashed up things and creatures and then retreated back into their money or their vast carelessness, or whatever it was that kept them together, and let other people clean up the mess they had made." "The Diamond As Big As the Ritz" can have a happy ending for the two lovers because it is a fantasy; but the same plot reappears in *The Great Gatsby*, where for the first time it is surrounded by the real world of the 1920s and for the first time is carried through to what Fitzgerald regarded as its logical conclusion.[3]

There is a time in any true author's career when he suddenly becomes capable of doing his best work. He has found a fable that expresses his central truth and everything falls into place around it, so that his whole experience of life is available for use in his fiction. Something like that happened to Fitzgerald when he invented the story of Jimmy Gatz, otherwise known as Jay Gatsby, and it explains the richness and scope of what is in fact a short novel.

To put facts on record, *The Great Gatsby* is a book of about fifty thousand words, a comparatively small structure built of nine chapters like big blocks. The fifth chapter—Gatsby's meeting after many years with Daisy Buchanan—is the center of the narrative, as is proper; the seventh chapter is its climax. Each chapter consists of one or more dramatic scenes, sometimes with intervening passages of narration. The scenic method is one that Fitzgerald possibly learned from Edith Wharton, who had learned it from Henry James; at any rate, the book is technically in the Jamesian tradition (and Daisy Buchanan is named for James's Daisy Miller).

Part of the tradition is the device of having events observed by a "central consciousness," often a character who stands somewhat apart from the action and whose vision frames it for the reader. In this instance the observer plays a special role. Although Nick Carraway does not save or ruin Gatsby, his personality in itself provides an essential comment on all the other character. Nick stands for the older values that prevailed in the Midwest before the First World War. His family is not tremendously rich like the Buchanans, but it has a long-established and sufficient fortune, so that Nick is the only person in the book who has not been corrupted by seeking or spending money. He is so certain of his own values that he hesitates to criticize others, but when he does pass judgment—on Gatsby, on Jordan Baker, on the Buchanans—he speaks as for ages to come.

All the other characters belong to their own brief era of confused and dissolving standards, but they are affected by the era in different fashions. Each of them represents some particular variety of moral failure; Lionel Trilling says that they are "treated as if they were ideographs," a true observation; but the treatment does not detract from their reality as persons. Tom Buchanan is wealth brutalized by selfishness and arrogance; he looks for a mistress in the valley of ashes and finds an ignorant woman, Myrtle Wilson, whose raw vitality is like his own. Daisy Buchanan is the butterfly soul of wealth and offers a continual promise "that she had done gay, exciting things just a while since and that there were gay, exciting things hovering in the next hour"; but it is a false promise, since at heart she is as self-centered as Tom and even colder. Jordan Baker apparently lives by the old standards, but she uses them only as a subterfuge. Aware of her own cowardice and dishonesty, she feels "safer on a plane where any divergence from a code would be thought impossible."

All these except Myrtle Wilson are East Egg people, that is, they are part of a community where wealth takes the form of solid possessions. Set against them are the West Egg people, whose wealth is fluid income that might cease to flow. The West Egg people, with Gatsby as their tragic hero, have worked furiously to rise in the world, but they will never reach East Egg for all the money they spend; at most they can sit at the water's edge and look across the bay at the green light that shines and promises at the end of the Buchanans' dock. The symbolism of place plays a great part in *Gatsby*, as does that of motorcars. The characters are visibly represented by the cars they drive: Nick has a conservative old Dodge, the Buchanans, too rich for ostentation, have an "easy-going blue coupé," and Gatsby's car is "a rich cream color, bright with nickel, swollen here and there in its monstrous length with triumphant hat-boxes and supper-boxes and tool-boxes, and terraced with a labyrinth of wind-shields that mirrored a dozen suns"—it is West Egg on wheels. When Daisy drives the monster through the valley of ashes, she runs down and kills Myrtle Wilson; then, by concealing her guilt, she causes the death of Gatsby.

The symbols are not synthetic or contrived, as are many of those in more recent novels; they are images that Fitzgerald instinctively found to represent his characters and their destiny. When he says, "Daisy took her face in her hands as if feeling its lovely shape," he is watching her act the charade of her self-love. When he says, "Tom would drift on forever seeking, a little wistfully, for the dramatic turbulence of some irrecoverable football game," he suggests the one appealing side of Tom's nature. The author is so familiar with the characters and their background, so absorbed in their fate, that the book has an admirable unity of texture; we can open it to any page and find another of the details that illuminate the story. We end by feeling that *Gatsby* has a double value: it is the best picture we possess of the age in which it was written, and it also achieves a sort of moral permanence. Fitzgerald's story of the suitor betrayed by the princess and murdered in his innocence is a fable of the 1920s that has survived as a legend for other times.

EDWIN S. FUSSELL

Fitzgerald's Brave New World

> Think of the lost ecstasy of the Elizabethans.
> "Oh my America, my new found land," think
> of what it meant to them and of what it means
> to us.
> (T. E. Hulme, *Speculations*)

I

Ultimately, Fitzgerald's literary stature derives from his ability to apply the sensibilities implied by the phrase "romantic wonder" to American civilization, and to gain from the conjunction a moral critique of that civilization. As this predominant motive took shape in Fitzgerald's writing, he approached and achieved an almost archetypal pattern that can be isolated and analyzed, admired for its aesthetic complexity and interest and valued for its ethical and social insight. Certainly, this pattern does not run through all Fitzgerald's fiction; but its significance is underscored by the fact that it appears in his two finest novels and in several of the best stories. It is important to us, because it embodies above all Fitzgerald's understanding of the past and the present—perhaps the future—of his America.

Fussell, Edwin S. "Fitzgerald's Brave New World". English Literary History 19:4 (1952), 291–306. © The John Hopkins University Press. Reprinted by permission of the John Hopkins University Press.

Fitzgerald's story, roughly, is of the New World, or, more exactly, of the work of the imagination in the New World. It has two predominant patterns, quest and seduction. The quest is the search for romantic wonder, in the terms which contemporary America offers for such a search; the seduction represents capitulation to these terms. Obversely, the quest is a flight: from reality, from normality, from time, fate, and the conception of *limit*. In the social realm, the pattern of desire may be suggested by the phrases "the American dream" and "the pursuit of happiness." Fitzgerald begins by showing the corruption of that dream in industrial America; he ends by discovering that the dream is universally seductive and perpetually unreal. Driven by forces that compel him towards the realization of romantic wonder, the Fitzgerald hero is destroyed by the materials which the American experience offers as objects of passion; or, at best, he is purged of these unholy fires, and chastened.

In general, this quest has two symbolic goals. There is, for one, the search for eternal youth and beauty, the myth of Ponce de Leon. (It is a curious coincidence that Frederick Jackson Turner used the image of "a magic fountain of youth" to describe the unexhausted frontier). The essence of romantic wonder appears to inhere in the illusion of perennial youth and grace created by the leisure class of which Fitzgerald usually wrote; thus the man of imagination in America is seduced by his illusion that these qualities inhere in a class that is charming, vacuous, and irresponsible. This kind of romantic quest which becomes escape is equated further, on the level of national ideology, with a transcendental and Utopian rejection of time and history and, on the religious level which Fitzgerald persistently but hesitantly approaches, with a blashemous rejection of the very condition of human existence.

The second goal is, simply enough, money. The search for money is the familiar American commercial ideal of personal materialistic success, most succinctly embodied for our culture in the saga of Benjamin Franklin. It is the romantic assumption of this aspect of the "American dream" that all the magic of the world can be had for money. Largely from the standpoint of the middle-class radicalism of the American progressive tradition, Fitzgerald examines and condemns the plutocratic ambitions of American life and the ruinous price exacted by this dream. But the two dreams are, of course, so intimately related as to be one: the appearance of eternal youth and beauty is centered in a particular social class whose glamor is made possible by a corrupt social inequality. Beauty, the object of aesthetic contemplation, is commercialized, love is bought and sold. Money is the means to the violent recovery of an enchanting lost youth. It is no accident that the word "pander" turns up in the key passage of *The Great Gatsby*.

In contrast, Fitzgerald affirms his faith repeatedly in an older, simpler America: the emotion is that of pastoral, the social connotations agrarian and democratic. In such areas Fitzgerald continues to find fragments of basic human value, social, moral, and religious. But these affirmations are largely subordinate and indirect: Fitzgerald's attention was primarily directed to the symbolism of romantic wonder proffered by his time and place and, like the narrator of *Gatsby*, he was "within and without, simultaneously enchanted and repelled by the inexhaustible variety of life." Through a delicate and exact symbolism, he was able to extend this attitude of simultaneous enchantment and repulsion over the whole of the American civilization he knew. His keenest perception was the universal quality of the patterns he had been tracing, his greatest discovery that there was nothing new about the Lost Generation except its particular symbols. The quest for romantic wonder and the inevitable failure were only the latest in a long series. It was thus that Fitzgerald conceived the tragedy of the American experience.

Fitzgerald approached this major theme slowly and more by intuition than design. In a hazy form it is present in such early stories as "The Offshore Pirate" and "Dalyrimple Goes Wrong." It is allegorized in "The Diamond as Big as the Ritz" and fumbled in *The Beautiful and Damned.*

But it is "May Day," significantly motivated by Fitzgerald's first sharp awareness of American society, which is, for one tracing Fitzgerald's gradual realization of this major theme, the most illuminating production of his early career. Its formal construction on social principles ("Mr. In" and "Mr. Out") is obvious enough; what has not been sufficiently remarked is the way Fitzgerald's symbolic method extends his critique from the manners of drunken undergraduates to the pervasive malaise of a whole civilization. The hubris with which these characters fade from the story may be taken as an example of how dramatically the story indicts the materialistic hedonism and the vulgar idealism that Fitzgerald is diagnosing as American shortcomings:

> Then they were in an elevator bound skyward.
> "What floor, please?" said the elevator man.
> "Any floor," said Mr. In.
> "Top floor," said Mr. Out.
> "This is the top floor," said the elevator man.
> "Have another floor put on," said Mr. Out.
> "Higher," said Mr. In.
> "Heaven," said Mr. Out.

Set against the tale's controlling symbol, the universal significance of this passage frames its particular historical implications. The scene is an all-night restaurant, and the preliminary setting emphasizes social and economic inequality, the brutalization of poverty and the apparent wonder of wealth. As a Yale junior is ejected for throwing hash at the waiters, "the great plate-glass front had turned to a deep creamy blue. . . Dawn had come up in Columbus Circle, magical, breathless dawn, silhouetting the great statue of the immortal Christopher, and mingling in a curious and uncanny manner with the fading yellow electric light inside." The final significance of the symbol can only be established after one considers the conclusion of *The Great Gatsby*, but the intention is clear enough: Fitzgerald is measuring the attitudes and behavior of the Lost Generation by means of a symbol of romantic wonder that is extensive enough to comprehend all American experience. The contrast amounts to the ironic rejection of all that this generation believes in, the immaturity and irresponsibility of its quest for "experience," when such a quest is juxtaposed with one (Columbus') that suggests the fullest possibilities for romantic wonder. There is the added implication that some kind of conscious search for experience is at the heart of American cultural history, but that the quest had never taken so childish a form. This, Fitzgerald seems to be saying, is what has become of Columbus' dream—this is our brave new world.

II

With *The Great Gatsby* (1925), Fitzgerald first brought his vision of America to full and mature realization. Notwithstanding its apparent lack of scope, this is a complex and resonant novel, and one with a variety of significant implications. No single reading, perhaps, will exhaust its primary meanings, and that which follows makes no pretense of doing so. But there is, I think, a central pattern that has never been sufficiently explored—this pattern is the story of America, or of the New World, the story that Fitzgerald had been intuitively approaching since he began to write.

Gatsby is essentially the man of imagination in America, given specificity and solidity and precision by the materials which American society offered him. "If personality is a series of successful gestures, then there was something gorgeous about him, some heightened sensitivity to the promises of life, as if he were related to one of those intricate machines that register earthquakes ten thousand miles away." It is Gatsby's capacity for *romantic wonder* that Fitzgerald is insisting upon in this preliminary exposition, a capacity that he goes on to define as "an extraordinary gift for hope, a romantic readiness." And with the simile of the seismograph, an apt enough symbol for the human sensibility in a mechanized age, Fitzgerald has in effect already introduced the vast back-drop of American civilization against which Gatsby's gestures must be interpreted. The image is as integral as intricate; for if Gatsby is to be taken as the product and the manifestation of those motivations caught up in the phrase "the American dream," he is also the instrument by means of which Fitzgerald is to register the tremors that point to its self-contained principles of destruction. "What preyed on Gatsby, what foul dust floated in the wake of his dreams" is ostensibly the stuff of the novel, the social content of Fitzgerald's universe of fiction. But it is essential to realize that Gatsby, too, has been distorted from the normative by values and attitudes that he holds in common with the society that destroys him. Certainly, in such a world, the novel assures us, a dream like Gatsby's cannot remain pristine, given the materials upon which the original impulse toward wonder must expend itself. Gatsby, in other words, is more than pathetic, a sad figure preyed upon by the American leisure class. The unreal values of the world of Tom and Daisy Buchanan are his values too, they are inherent in his dream. Gatsby had always lived in an imaginary world, where "a universe of ineffable gaudiness spun itself out in his brain"; negatively, this quality manifests itself in a dangerous tendency toward sentimental idealization: his reveries "were a satisfactory hint of the unreality of reality, a promise that the rock of the world was founded securely on a fairy's wing."

Daisy finally becomes for Gatsby the iconic manifestation of this vision of beauty. Little enough might have been possible for Gatsby anyway, but once he "wed his unutterable visions to her perishable breath, his mind would never romp again like the mind of God." One notes how steadily if surreptitiously, through his metaphors and similes mainly, Fitzgerald is introducing the notion of blasphemy in conjunction with Gatsby's Titanic imaginative lusts. But the novel makes only tentative gestures in the direction of religious evaluation; Fitzgerald's talent indicated that Gatsby's visions be focussed rather sexually and socially. After this concentration of Gatsby's wonder on Daisy has been established, Fitzgerald can go on to an explicit statement of her significance to the thematic direction of the novel: Gatsby, we are told, was "overwhelmingly aware of the *youth* and mystery that *wealth* imprisons and *preserves*, of the freshness of many clothes, and of Daisy, gleaming like silver, safe and proud above the hot struggle of the poor" (my italics). Her voice is frequently mentioned as mysteriously enchanting—it is the typifying feature of her role as *la belle dame sans merci*—and throughout the action it serves to suggest her loveliness and desirability. But only Gatsby, in a rare moment of vision, is able to make explicit the reasons for its subtle and elusive magic: "It was full of money—that was the inexhaustible charm that rose and fell in it, the jingle of it, the cymbal's song of it . . . High in a while palace the king's daughter, the golden girl. . . ."

Possession of an image like Daisy is all that Gatsby can finally conceive as "success"; and Gatsby is meant to be a very representative American in the intensity of his yearning for success, as well as in the symbols which he equates with it. Gatsby performs contemporary variations on an old American pattern, the rags-to-riches story exalted by American legend as early as Crevecoeur's *Letters from an American Farmer*. But the saga is primarily that of a legendary Benjamin Franklin, whose celebrated youthful resolutions are parodied in those that the adolescent Gatsby wrote on the back flyleaf of his copy of *Hopalong Cassidy*. As an indictment of American philistinism, Fitzgerald's burlesque is spare and sharp; what accounts for its impression of depth is Fitzgerald's fictionally realized perception that Gatsby's was not a unique, but a pervasive American social pattern. Grounding his parody in Franklin's *Autobiography* gave Fitzgerald's critique a historical density and a breadth of implication that one associates only with major fiction.

The connection between Gatsby's individual tragedy and the tragedy of his whole civilization is also made (and again, through symbol) with respect to historical attitudes. Gatsby's relation to history is summed up in his devotion to the green light that burns on Daisy's dock. When Nick first sees Gatsby, he is in an attitude of supplication, a gesture that pathetically travesties the gestures of worship; Nick finally observes that the object of his trembling piety is this green light which, until his disillusion, is one of Gatsby's "enchanted objects." In the novel's concluding passage, toward which all action and symbol is relentlessly tending, one is given finally the full implications of the green light as symbol ("Gatsby believed in the green light, the orgiastic future").

Gatsby, with no historical sense whatsoever, is the fictional counterpart of that American philistine maxim that "history is bunk"; and he may recall, too, for those interested in such comparisons, the more crowing moods of Emerson and Thoreau, and the "timelessness" of their visions and exhortations. But for Fitzgerald, this contemptuous repudiation of tradition, historical necessity, and moral determinism, however un-self-conscious, was deluded and hubristic. When he finally came to see, as he did in *Gatsby*, that in this irresponsibility lay the real meaning behind the American obsession with youth, he was able to know Gatsby as a miserable, twentieth century Ponce de Leon. And his fictional world was no longer simply the Jazz Age, the Lost Generation, but the whole of American civilization as it culminated in his own time.

In the final symbol of the book, Fitzgerald pushes the personal equation to national, even universal, scope, and in a way that recalls the method of "May Day." The passage has been prepared for in multiple ways; indeed, nearly all the material I have been citing leads directly into it. Even the "new world" theme has been anticipated. Fitzgerald is commenting on Gatsby's state of disillusion just before his death: he must have felt that he had lost the old warm world, paid a high price for living too long with a single dream. He must have looked up at an unfamiliar sky through frightening leaves and shivered as he found what a grotesque thing a rose is and how raw the sunlight was upon the scarcely created grass. A new world, material without being real, where poor ghosts, breathing dreams like air, drifted fortuitously about . . .

Such, then, was the romantic perception of wonder, when finally stripped of its falsifying illusions. Gatsby finds himself in a "new world" (Fitzgerald's symbol for the American's dream of irresponsibility takes on ironically terrifying overtones here) in which his values and dreams are finally exposed. And so Fitzgerald moves on to his final critique:

> And as the moon rose higher the inessential houses began to melt away until gradually I became aware of the old island here that flowered once for Dutch sailors' eyes—a fresh green breast of the new world. Its vanished trees, the trees that had made way for Gatsby's house, had once pandered in whispers to the last and greatest of all human dreams; for a transitory enchanted moment man must have held his breath in the presence of this continent, compelled into an aesthetic contemplation he neither understood nor desired, face to face for the last time in history with something commensurate to his capacity for wonder.

The most important point to be made about this passage is its insistence that Gatsby's abnormal capacity for wonder could have, in the modern world, no proper objective. The emotion lingered on, generations of Americans had translated it into one or another set of inadequate terms, but Gatsby, like all his ancestors, was doomed by demanding the impossible. There is, too, the ironic contrast between the wonder of the New World, and what Americans have made of it (the same point that Fitzgerald made in similar fashion with the Columbus image in "May Day"). But there is a final, more universal meaning, implicit in the language of the passage—the hope that the new world could possibly satisfy man's lusts was, after all, "the last and greatest of all human dreams," unreal. The most impressive associations cluster around the word "pander"—a word that implies, above all, the illicit commercialization of love, youth, and beauty—which effectually subsumes most of the central meanings of the novel. Because of the verbal similarity, it is valuable to compare this phrase "panders in whispers" with Fitzgerald's remarks (in "My Lost city" [1932], an essay collected in 1945 in *The Crack-Up*) about New York City, a good instance of how the myths of Benjamin Franklin and Ponce de Leon could be blended in his mind—"it no longer whispers of fantastic success and eternal youth." The two parallel themes do, of course, come together in the novel; in fact, they are tangled at the heart of the plot, for the greatest irony in Gatsby's tragedy is his belief that he can buy his dream, which is, precisely, to recapture the past.

III

Tender is the Night (1934) at once restates the essential theme and complicates it. Because of the greater proliferation of symbolic statement here, it is less easy to define the novel's main designs, and yet they are remarkably parallel to those already traced out for *The Great Gatsby*. This becomes apparent if one examines carefully the implications of the leading characters and the meaning of their narrative; attention to the metaphoric and symbolic overtones of the novel further corroborates the impression that, beneath this greater wealth of detail, Fitzgerald is still telling the same story.

Dick Diver is, like Gatsby, the American as man of imagination. His chief difference from Gatsby is that he dispenses romantic wonder to others, in addition to living for it himself; Gatsby tries to purvey dreams, but doesn't know how. But to Rosemary Hoyt, Dick's "voice promised that he would take care of her, and that a little later he would open up whole *new worlds* for her, unroll an endless succession of magnificent possibilities" (my italics). Dick is the man with the innate capacity for romantic wonder, but now a member of the American leisure class of the 'twenties, now declined to an "organizer of private gaiety, curator of a richly incrusted happiness." His intellectual and imaginative energies have been diverted from the normal creative channels they might have taken and are expended on the effort to prevent, for a handful of the very rich, the American dream from revealing its nightmarish realities.

Although Dick is given a more positive background than Gatsby, he is equally a product of his civilization and he has its characteristic deficiencies: "The illusions of eternal strength and health, and of the essential goodness of people; illusions of a nation, the lies of generations of frontier mothers who had to croon falsely that there were no wolves at the cabin door." And this inherent romantic has been further weakened by the particular forms of sentimentality of his own generation: "he must press on toward the Isles of Greece, the cloudy waters of unfamiliar ports, the lost girl on shore, the moon of the popular songs. A part of Dick's mind was made up of the tawdry souvenirs of his boyhood. Yet in that somewhat littered Five-and-Ten, he had managed to keep alive the low painful fire of intelligence.'"

Such is the man, essentially noble like Gatsby, but with the fatal flaw of imagination common to and conditioned by the superficial symbols and motivations of his civilization, who is brought against the conditions of temptation represented by Nicole. She is the granddaughter of a "self-made American capitalist" and of a German Count, and her family is placed in perspective by Fitzgerald's frequent analogies with a feudal aristocracy. "Her father would have it on almost any clergyman," such as Dick's father; "they were an American ducal family without a title—the very name . . . caused a psychological metamorphosis in people." Yet behind this facade of glamour and power lies unnatural lust and perversion. Nicole's father, this "fine American type," has committed incest with his daughter—the very incarnation of the American vision of youth, beauty, and wealth—and made her into a psychotic whom young Dr. Diver must cure. As Nicole says, "I'm a crook by heritage."

Through Nicole, Fitzgerald conveys, as he had with Daisy, all that is sexually and socially desirable in youth and beauty: "there were all the potentialities for romantic love in that lovely body and in the delicate mouth. . . . Nicole had been a beauty as a young girl and she would be a beauty later." Apparently she is eternally youthful, and only at the end of the novel is it discernible that she has aged. Her face, which corresponds in symbolic utility to Daisy's voice, is lovely and hard, "her eyes brave and watchful, looking straight ahead at nothing." She is an empty child, representative of her social class, of the manners and morals of the 'twenties, and of the world of values for which America, like Dick, was once more selling its soul. But it is, more than anything else, Nicole's semblance of perpetual youth that allows Fitzgerald to exploit her as a central element in the narrative correlative he is constructing for his vision of American life. Occasionally, there is a treatment of Nicole that goes beyond social criticism, entering, if obliquely and implicitly, the area of religious vision:

> The only physical disparity between Nicole at present and the Nicole of five years before was simply that she was no longer a young girl. But she was enough ridden by the current youth worship, the moving pictures with their myriad faces of girl-children, blandly represented as carrying on the work and wisdom of the world, to feel a jealousy of youth. She put on the first ankle-length day dress that she had owned for many years, and crossed herself reverently with Chanel Sixteen.

But while Fitzgerald could upon occasion so extend the significance of his narrative, he never neglected to keep it firmly grounded in a specific social and economic world, and it is in this realm that most of his correspondences are established:

> Nicole was the product of much ingenuity and toil. For her sake trains began their run at Chicago and traversed the round belly of the continent to California; chicle factories fumed and link belts grew link by link in factories; men mixed toothpaste in vats and drew mouthwash out of copper hogsheads; girls canned tomatoes quickly in August or worked rudely at the Five-and-Tens on Christmas Eve; half-breed Indians toiled on Brazilian coffee plantations and dreamers were muscled out of patient rights in new tractors—these were some of the people who gave a tithe to Nicole, and as the whole system swayed and thundered onward it lent a feverish bloom to such processes of hers as wholesale buying, like the flush of a fireman's face holding his post before a spreading blaze. She illustrated very simple principles, containing in herself her own doom, but illustrated them so accurately that there was grace in the procedure.

The social structure of *Tender Is The Night* is epic in scope and intention, though it has the grace and concentration of lyric; at its base are criminal injustice and inhuman waste—at its apex is Nicole, "the king's daughter"—beautiful, forever young, and insane.

In the central scenes of temptation (Book II, chapter v), Fitzgerald quite deliberately allows Nicole to expand into her full symbolic significance, thus revealing that the larger thematic pattern of *Tender Is the Night* must be read against the largest context of American life. Throughout the chapter runs the *leitmotif* of Fitzgerald's generalizing commentary, beginning with the passage: "the impression of her youth and beauty grew on Dick until it welled up inside him in a compact paroxysm of emotion. She smiled, a moving childish smile that was like all the lost youth in the world." This mood of pathetic nostalgia is quickly objectified in the talk of Dick and Nicole about American popular songs; soon Dick feels that "there was that excitement about her that seemed to reflect all the excitement of the world." So ends the first of the two scenes that form this chapter. The second meeting of the two opens on a similar key: "Dick wished she had no background, that she was just a girl lost with no address save the night from which she had come." This time they play the songs they had mentioned the week before, "they were in America now." And Fitzgerald drives home the point in his last sentence: "Now there was this scarcely saved waif of disaster bringing him the essence of a continent. . . ."

At first Dick laughs off the notion that Nicole's family has bought him, but he gradually succumbs, "inundated by a trickling of goods and money." And Nicole is, once more, the typifying object of her class and society in the particular terms she imposes for the destruction of his moral and intellectual integrity: "Naturally Nicole, *wanting to own him, wanting him to stand still forever*, encouraged any slackness on his part" (my italics). And so, although the pattern is more complex than in *Gatsby*, practically the same controlling lines of theme can be observed. The man of imagination, fed on the emotions of romantic wonder, is tempted and seduced and (in this case, nearly) destroyed by the American dream which customarily takes two forms: the escape from time and the materialistic pursuit of a purely hedonistic happiness. On the historical level, the critique is of the error of American romanticism in attempting to transcend and escape historical responsibility. On the economic level, the critique is of the fatal beauty of American capitalism, its destructive charm and irresponsibility. And on the level of myth, one need mention only the names of Benjamin Franklin and Ponce de Leon to recall the motivations of the quest that Fitzgerald recurrently explores. Thematically, the lines come together when Nicole attempts to own Dick and therefore escape Time, as when Gatsby tries to buy back the past.

It is Fitzgerald's skill in elaborating a more complicated symbolization of unreality that makes *Tender is the Night* more impressive than *The Great Gatsby*. In Rosemary Hoyt, who brings from Hollywood to Europe the latest American version of the dream of youth and innocence, Fitzgerald has another important symbol and center of consciousness. It is through her perception, for instance, that Fitzgerald gives us his first elaborate glimpses of the Divers and of the American leisure class. Because of Rosemary's acute but undisciplined perceptions, Fitzgerald can insist perpetually on the ironic tensions between the richest texture of social appearance and the hidden reality of social evil; her "naivete responded whole-heartedly to the expensive simplicity of the Divers, unaware of its complexity and its lack of innocence, unaware that it was all a selection of quality rather than quantity from the run of the world's bazaar; and that the simplicity of behavior, also, the nursery-like peace and good will, the emphasis on the simpler virtues, was part of a desperate bargain with the gods and had been attained through struggles she could not have guessed at."

Rosemary manifests the effects of Hollywood sentimentality and meretriciousness on the powers of American perception and imagination. The image-patterns that surround her movement are largely concerned with childhood; she is "as dewy with belief as a child from one of Mrs. Burnett's vicious tracts." Immature and egocentric, she provides one more symbol of the corruption of imagination by American civilization; both deluded and deluding, she has no opportunity for escape, as there is for Nick Carroway and Dick Diver. It is Diver who sounds the last important note about her: "'Rosemary didn't grow up.'" That she is intended symbolically, Fitzgerald makes clear in his account of her picture "Daddy's Girl": "There she was— *so* young and innocent—the product of her mother's loving care; embodying all the immaturity of the race, cutting a new cardboard paper doll to pass before its empty harlot's mind."

Nicole and Rosemary, then, are for this novel the objectified images of Fitzgerald's "brave new world." Only occasionally does Dick Diver escape the limits of this terrifying world. Once, the three of them are sitting in a restaurant, and Dick observes a group of "gold star mothers": "in their happy faces, the dignity that surrounded and pervaded the party he perceived all the maturity of an Older America. For a while the sobered women who had come to mourn for their dead, for something they could not repair, made the room beautiful. Momentarily, he sat again on his father's knee, riding with Moseby while the old loyalties and devotions fought on around him. Almost with an effort he turned back to his two women at the table and faced the whole new world in which he believed." In the gradual failure of this illusion comes Dick Diver's salvation; as the dream fades, he is enabled to recover a fragment of reality.

IV

For purposes of corroboration, one can add a certain amount of documentation from Fitzgerald's non-fictional writings, as collected in the posthumous *Crack-Up*. And the point that most needs buttressing, probably, is that Fitzgerald saw in the quest for romantic wonder a recurrent pattern of American behavior. This attitude seems strongly implied by the stories themselves, but it is additionally reassuring to find Fitzgerald writing, in a letter to his daughter: "You speak of how good your generation is, but I think they share with every generation since the Civil War in America the sense of being somehow about to inherit the earth. You've heard me say before that I think the faces of most American women over thirty are relief maps of petulant and bewildered unhappiness" (p. 306). A brief sketch of a "typical product of our generation" in the *Note-Books* indicates further what qualities were involved in this "sense of being about to inherit the earth": "her dominant idea and *goal* is *freedom without responsibility*, which is like *gold* without metal, spring without winter, *youth without age*, one of those maddening, coocoo *mirages of wild riches*" (p. 166—my italics). And that this personal attitude, translated into the broader terms of a whole culture, represented a negation of historical responsibility is made sufficiently clear in another *Note-Book* passage: "Americans, he liked to say, needed fins and wings. There was even a *recurrent idea* in should be born with fins, and perhaps they were—perhaps money was a form of fin. In England, property begot a strong place sense, but Americans, restless and with shallow roots, America about an education that would leave out history and the past, that should be a sort of equipment for aerial adventure, weighed down by none of the stowaways of inheritance or tradition" (p. 109—my italics). Still another passage, this time from one of the "Crack-Up" essays, makes it equally clear that Fitzgerald habitually saw the universal applicability of all he was saying about the ruling passion in America: "This is what I think now: that the natural state of the sentient adult is a qualified unhappiness. I think also that in an adult the desire to be finer in grain than you are, 'a constant striving' (as those people say who gain their bread by saying it) only adds to this unhappiness in the end—that end that comes to our youth and hope" (p. 80).

And yet, for all the failure and futility that Fitzgerald found in the American experience, his attitude remained one of acceptance, and not one of despair. There was no cynicism in his "wise and tragic sense of life." The exhaustion of the frontier and the post-war expatriate movement marked for him the end of a long period in human history and it was this period, the history of the post-Renaissance European man in America, that he made his subject. After he had explored his materials to their limits Fitzgerald knew, at his greatest moments, that he had discovered in an archetypal pattern of desire and belief and behavior compounded the imaginative history of modern civilization. One final passage from the *Note-Books* may substantiate our impression that Fitzgerald could, on occasion, conceive his subject in all the range and heroism of the epic mode:

> He felt then that if the pilgrimage eastward of the rare poisonous flower of his race was the end of the adventure which had started westward three hundred years ago, if the long serpent of the curiosity had turned too sharp upon itself, cramping its bowels, bursting its shining skin, at least there had been a journey; like to the satisfaction of a man coming to die—one of those human things that one can never understand unless one has made such a journey and heard the man give thanks with the husbanded breath. The frontiers were gone—there were no more barbarians. The short gallop of the last great race, the polyglot, the hated and the despised, the crass and scorned, had gone—at least it was not a meaningless extinction up an alley.

Chronology

1896 Francis Scott Key Fitzgerald is born in St. Paul, Minnesota, on September 24

1901 Family moves to Syracuse; sister Annabel is born

1908 Family returns to St. Paul; Scott enters St. Paul Academy

1911 Scott is sent to Newman Academy in New Jersey

1913 Scott enters Princeton

1914 Scott meets Ginevra King

1915 Scott leaves the university and returns to St. Paul

1917 Scott receives commission as infantry 2nd lieutenant; reports to Fort Leavenworth, Kansas, for officer's training

1918 Scott finishes first draft of *The Romantic Egotist*; meets Zelda Sayre

1919 Discharged from army; goes to New York; takes job with Barron Collier Advertising Agency; returns to St. Paul to finish novel; sells first story to *Saturday Evening Post*

1920 *This Side of Paradise* published; Scott and Zelda are married

1921 First trip to Europe; Scottie born in St. Paul

1922 *The Beautiful and Damned* published in April; *Tales of the Jazz Age* published in September

1923 Scott's play *The Vegetable* fails in Atlantic City

1924 Fitzgeralds move to Europe; meet Gerald Murphy; *The Great Gatsby* is published

1926 *All the Sad Young Men* published; Fitzgeralds return to America

1927 Fitzgeralds' first trip to Hollywood; move to Ellerslie near Wilmington, Delaware

1928 Fitzgeralds go to Paris for the summer; return to Ellerslie in the fall.

1929 Fitzgeralds return to France; Zelda studies ballet

1930 Zelda breaks down and is hospitalized in Switzerland

1931 Scott's father dies and Scott returns to America in January; Fitzgeralds return to live in Montgomery in September; Scott returns to Hollywood in November

1932 Zelda's father dies; she suffers another breakdown, admitted to Johns Hopkins; Scott moves to Baltimore

1934 *Tender Is the Night* published; Zelda suffers third breakdown

1935 *Taps at Reveille* is published

1936 Scott's mother dies, leaving inheritance

1937 Scott returns to Hollywood; gets contract with MGM; meets Sheilah Graham

1938 Contract with MGM not renewed in December

1939 Scott writes first chapter of *The Last Tycoon*

1940 Scott dies of a heart attack

1948 Zelda dies in a fire at Asheville Hospital

Works by F. Scott Fitzgerald

This Side of Paradise
The Beautiful and Damned
The Great Gatsby
Tender Is the Night
Taps at Reveille
The Last Tycoon
The Stories of F. Scott Fitzgerald
Afternoon of an Author
Flappers and Philosophers
Babylon Revisited and Other Stories
Six Tales of the Jazz Age and Other Stories
The Pat Hobby Stories

Works about F. Scott Fitzgerald

Berman, Ronald. The Great Gatsby and Modern Times. Urbana, Illinois: University of Illinois Press, 1994.

Bloom, Harold, ed. Modern Critical Views: F. Scott Fitzgerald. New York: Chelsea House, 1985.

Burton, Mary E. "The Counter-Transference of Dr. Driver." English Literary History. 38, no. 3 (1971): 459-471.

Bruccoli, Matthew J. Classes on F. Scott Fitzgerald. Columbia, South Carolina: University of South Carolina, 2001.

————., editor. Collected Writings of Zelda Fitzgerald. New York: Scribner, 1991.

Callahan, John. F. The Illusions of a Nation: Myth and History in the Novels F. Scott Fitzgerald. Urbana, Illinois: University of Illinois Press, 1972.

Carpenter, Humphrey. Geniuses Together: American Writers in Paris in the 1920s. Boston: Houghton Mifflin, 1988.

Cowley, Malcolm. A Second Flowering: Works and Days of the Lost Generation. New York: Viking, 1973.

Fraser, John. "Dust and Dreams in The Great Gatsby." English Literary History. 32, no. 4 (1965): 554-564.

Fussell, Edwin S. "Fitzgerald's Brave New World." English Literary History. 19, no. 4 (1952): 291-306.

Graham, Sheilah, and Frank, Gerold. Beloved Infidel. New York: Holt, Rinehart & Winston, 1958.

Hansen, Arlen J. *Expatriate Paris: A Cultural and Literary Guide to Paris in the 1920s.* New York: Arcade Publishers, 1990.

Hindus, Milton. *F. Scott Fitzgerald: An Introduction and Interpretation.* New York: Holt, Rinehart and Winston, 1968.

Kerr, Frances. "Feeling 'Half Feminine': Modernism and the Politics of Emotion in *The Great Gatsby.*" *American Literature.* 68, no. 2 (1996): 405-431.

Korenman, Joan S. "'Only Her Hairdresser…': Another Look at Daisy Buchanan." *American Literature.* 46, no. 4 (1975): 574-578.

Kuehl, John and Bryer, Jackson, editors. *Dear Scott/Dear Max: The Fitzgerald-Perkins Correspondence.* New York: Charles Scribner's Sons, 1971.

Lanahan, Eleanor Anne. *Scottie: the daughter of F. Scott Fitzgerald: the life of Frances Scott Fitzgerald Lanahan Smith.* New York: Harper Collins, 1995.

Lehan, Richard. *F. Scott Fitzgerald and the Craft of Fiction.* Carbondale: Southern Illinois University Press, 1966.

Michaels, Walter Benn. *Our America: Nativism, Modernism, and Pluralism.* Durham, North Carolina: Duke University Press, 1995.

Milford, Nancy. *Zelda.* New York: Harper & Row, 1970.

Mizener, Arthur. *The Far Side of Paradise: A Biography of F. Scott Fitzgerald.* Boston: Houghton Mifflin Company, 1951.

Pelzer, Linda C. *Student Companion to F. Scott Fitzgerald.* Westport, Connecticut: Greenwood Press, 2000.

Person, Leland S. "'Herstory' and Daisy Buchanan." *American Literature.* 50, no. 2 (1978): 250-257.

Piper, Henry Dan. *Fitzgerald's The Great Gatsby: The Novel, The Critics, The Background.* New York: Scribner, 1970.

———. *F. Scott Fitzgerald: A Critical Portrait.* New York: Holt, Rinehart and Winston, 1965.

Seiters, Dan. *Image Patterns in the Novels of F. Scott Fitzgerald.* Ann Arbor: UMI Research Press, 1986.

Stern, Milton R. *The Golden Moment: The Novels of F. Scott Fitzgerald.* Urbana, Illinois: University of Illinois Press, 1970.

Tate, Mary Jo, and Brucoli, Matthew J. *F. Scott Fitzgerald A to Z*. New York: Checkmark Books, 1999.

Toles, George. "The Metaphysics of Style in *Tender Is the Night*." *American Literature*. 62, no. 3 (1990): 423-444.

Trachtenberg, Alan. "The Journey Back: Myth and History in *Tender Is the Night*." In *Critical Essay on F. Scott Fitzgerald's Tender is the Night*, edited by Milton R. Stern. Boston: G. K. Hall & Co, 1986: 170-185.

Trilling, Lionel. *The Liberal Imagination: Essays on Literature and Society*. New York: Viking, 1950.

Turnbull, Andrew, editor. *The Letters of F. Scott Fitzgerald*. New York: Charles Scribner's Sons, 1963.

———, editor. *Scott Fitzgerald: Letters to His Daughter*. New York: Charles Scribner's Sons, 1963.

Way, Brian. *F. Scott Fitzgerald and the Art of Social Fiction*. New York: St. Martin's Press, 1980.

Wilson, Edmund. *The Shores of Light: A Literary Chronicle of the Twenties and Thirties*. New York: Farrar, Straus and Young, 1952.

Contributors

HAROLD BLOOM is Sterling Professor of the Humanities at Yale University and Henry W. and Albert A. Berg Professor of English at the New York University Graduate School. He is the author of over 20 books, including *Shelly's Mythmaking* (1959), *The Visionary Company* (1961), *Blake's Apocalypse* (1963), *Yeats* (1970), *A Map of Misreading* (1975), *Kabbalah and Criticism* (1975), *Agon: Toward a Theory of Revisionism* (1982), *The American Religion* (1992), *The Western Canon* (1994), and *Omens of Millennium: The Gnosis of Angels, Dreams, and Resurrection* (1996). *The Anxiety of Influence* (1973) sets forth Professor Bloom's provocative theory of the literary relationships between the great writers and their predecessors. His most recent books include *Shakespeare: The Invention of the Human*, a 1998 National Book Award finalist, and *How to Read and Why*, which was published in 2000. In 1999, Professor Bloom received the prestigious American Academy of Arts and Letters Gold Medal for Criticism.

NORMA JEAN LUTZ has been writing professionally since 1977. She is the author of more than 250 short stories and articles as well as 40-plus books—fiction and nonfiction.

THOMAS HEISE is a poet and a PhD candidate in English Literature at New York University. His poetry has appeared in *Indiana Review*, *Columbia: A Journal of Literature and Art*, *Southern Humanities Review*, and *The New York Quarterly*.

LIONEL TRILLING was one of the most influential critics of the post-World War II generation and a Professor at Columbia University. In addition to *The Liberal Imagination*, his books include *The Middle of the Journey* and *Sincerity and Authenticity*.

MALCOLM COWLEY, a literary critic, poet, editor, and historian—he was one of America's leading man of letters. He is best remembered for *Exile's Return* and *A Second Flowering*.

EDWIN S. FUSSELL is the author of *Edwin Arlington Robinson: The Literary Background of a Traditional Poet* and *Lucifer in Harness: American Meter, Metaphor and Diction*. He is Professor Emeritus of American Literature at the University of California, San Diego.

Notes

The Liberal Imagination

1 George Moore's comment on Æ's having spoken in reproof of Yeats's pride in a quite factitious family line is apposite; "Æ, who is usually quick-witted, should have guessed that Yeats's belief in his lineal descent from the great Duke of Ormonde was part of his poetic equipment."

The Romance of Money

1 Those sums of money should be multiplied by three to give a notion of their equivalents half a century later. Income taxes were low in the 1920s. By the end of the decade Fitzgerald would be spending as much—but not for the same things—as the presidents of small corporations.

2 For the complete invocation to drunkenness, see *Of Time and the River*, pp. 281–82. The novel is in the third person, but here, in celebrating what he regarded as a generational experience, Wolfe shifts to the first person plural.

[3] The plot appears for the last time in *Tender Is the Night*. "The novel should do this," Fitzgerald said in a memorandum to himself written early in 1932, after several false starts on the book and before setting to work on the published version. "Show a man who is a natural idealist, a spoiled priest, giving in for various causes to the ideas of the haute bourgeoisie"—that is, of the old moneyed class—"and in his rise to the top of the social world losing his idealism, his talent and turning to drink and dissipation." In the very simplest terms, Dick Diver marries Nicole Warren and is destroyed by her money.

Index